THE PSYCHOLOGY

Can mediums communicate with the dead? Do people really believe they've been abducted by aliens? Why do some people make life decisions based on their horoscope?

The Psychology of the Paranormal explores some commonly held beliefs regarding experiences so strange they can defy any obvious scientific explanation. The book explains how psychologists have conducted experiments to provide insight into phenomena such as clairvoyance, astrology, and alien abduction, as well as teaching us fundamental truths about human belief systems.

From debunking myths about extra-sensory perception to considering whether our lives can truly be fated by the stars, *The Psychology of the Paranormal* shows us that, however unlikely, belief in the paranormal will continue to be widespread.

David Groome was formerly Principal Lecturer in Psychology at the University of Westminster, UK. In 2009, he received the BPS Award for Excellence in the Teaching of Psychology.

Michael Eysenck is Professorial Fellow at Roehampton University and Emeritus Professor and Honorary Fellow at Royal Holloway, University of London, UK.

Robin Law is Senior Lecturer in Psychology at the University of Westminster, UK.

THE PSYCHOLOGY OF EVERYTHING

The Psychology of Everything is a series of books which debunk the myths and pseudo-science surrounding some of life's biggest questions.

The series explores the hidden psychological factors that drive us, from our sub-conscious desires and aversions to the innate social instincts handed to us across the generations. Accessible, informative, and always intriguing, each book is written by an expert in the field, examining how research-based knowledge compares with popular wisdom and illustrating the potential of psychology to enrich our understanding of humanity and modern life.

Applying a psychological lens to an array of topics and contemporary concerns – from sex to addiction to conspiracy theories – The Psychology of Everything will make you look at everything in a new way.

Titles in the series:

The Psychology of Grief
Richard Gross

The Psychology of Sex
Meg-John Barker

The Psychology of Dieting
Jane Ogden

The Psychology of Performance
Stewart T. Cotterill

The Psychology of Trust
Ken J. Rotenberg

The Psychology of Working Life
Toon W. Taris

The Psychology of Conspiracy Theories
Jan-Willem van Prooijen

The Psychology of Addiction
Jenny Svanberg

The Psychology of Fashion
Carolyn Mair

The Psychology of Gardening
Harriet Gross

The Psychology of Gender
Gary Wood

The Psychology of Climate Change
Geoffrey Beattie and Laura McGuire

The Psychology of Vampires
David Cohen

The Psychology of Chess
Fernand Gobet

The Psychology of Music
Susan Hallam

The Psychology of Weather
Trevor Harley

The Psychology of Driving
Graham J. Hole

The Psychology of Retirement
Doreen Rosenthal and Susan M. Moore

The Psychology of School Bullying
Peter Smith

The Psychology of Celebrity
Gayle Stever

The Psychology of Dog Ownership
Craig Roberts and Theresa Barlow

The Psychology of Social Media
Ciarán Mc Mahon

The Psychology of Happiness
Peter Warr

The Psychology of Politics
Barry Richards

The Psychology of the Paranormal
David Groome, Michael Eysenck, and Robin Law

For further information about this series please visit
www.thepsychologyofeverything.co.uk

THE PSYCHOLOGY OF THE PARANORMAL

DAVID GROOME, MICHAEL EYSENCK, AND ROBIN LAW

Routledge
Taylor & Francis Group
LONDON AND NEW YORK

First published 2019
by Routledge
2 Park Square, Milton Park, Abingdon, Oxon OX14 4RN

and by Routledge
711 Third Avenue, New York, NY 10017

Routledge is an imprint of the Taylor & Francis Group, an informa business

© 2019 David Groome, Michael Eysenck, and Robin Law

The right of David Groome, Michael Eysenck, and Robin Law to be identified as the authors of this work has been asserted by them in accordance with sections 77 and 78 of the Copyright, Designs and Patents Act 1988.

All rights reserved. No part of this book may be reprinted or reproduced or utilised in any form or by any electronic, mechanical, or other means, now known or hereafter invented, including photocopying and recording, or in any information storage or retrieval system, without permission in writing from the publishers.

Trademark notice: Product or corporate names may be trademarks or registered trademarks, and are used only for identification and explanation without intent to infringe.

British Library Cataloguing-in-Publication Data
A catalogue record for this book is available from the British Library

Library of Congress Cataloging-in-Publication Data
Names: Groome, David, 1946- author.
Title: The psychology of the paranormal / David Groome, Michael Eysenck, and Robin Law.
Description: 1 [edition]. | New York : Routledge, 2019. | Series: The psychology of everything
Identifiers: LCCN 2018057592 | ISBN 9781138307858 (hardback)
Subjects: LCSH: Parapsychology.
Classification: LCC BF1031 .G76 2019 | DDC 130—dc23
LC record available at https://lccn.loc.gov/2018057592

ISBN: 978-1-138-30785-8 (hbk)
ISBN: 978-1-138-30788-9 (pbk)
ISBN: 978-1-315-14262-3 (ebk)

Typeset in Joanna
by Apex CoVantage, LLC

Printed in Canada

CONTENTS

1	Introduction	1
2	Astrology	9
3	Extra-sensory perception	27
4	Spirits and mediums	41
5	Alien encounters and abductions	53
6	Religious beliefs	67
7	Explaining paranormal beliefs	85

1

INTRODUCTION

David Groome, Michael Eysenck, and Robin Law

STRANGE AND UNUSUAL EXPERIENCES

Many people believe that they have experienced events which are so strange that they defy any scientific explanation. Such experiences are referred to as "paranormal", because they cannot be explained by any normal processes known to science at the present time. It is possible that a scientific explanation might one day be found for these claims, but in the meantime some scientists prefer not to make any assumptions about paranormal causes and refer to such phenomena as merely "unusual experiences", strange events which we may one day be able to explain in some rational way.

The purpose of this book is to evaluate the scientific evidence supporting claims of paranormal experience and to consider the possible explanations for such phenomena. The main categories of unusual and paranormal experience will be examined in detail in the book, including the following:

Extra-sensory perception (ESP), which is also known as "telepathy" or "paranormal cognition" (and also The Sixth Sense, if you happened to see that movie). It refers to the perception of input through some channel other than the five main senses,

where a person appears to pick up information from other people by some unknown mechanism of transmission.
- *Mediums* claim to be able to contact the spirits of dead people, a claim which assumes that the dead continue to survive in spirit form and are able to communicate with living people (again, this features in *The Sixth Sense*, *Ghost*, and quite a few other films).
- *Alien contact* refers to alleged encounters with extra-terrestrial visitors (did you see *Close Encounters of the Third Kind*?). Some people believe they have met such visitors from outer space, and in some cases, they believe that they have actually been abducted by aliens for some purpose. These experiences are usually classified as paranormal because there is no convincing evidence that this planet has actually been visited by aliens.
- *Astrology* is based on the belief that the stars somehow influence people's lives, their character, and their destiny. Again, the mechanism by which this might occur remains unknown. Some authorities argue that astrology is not a true paranormal phenomenon as it does not involve any form of paranormal experience as such. However, we have included a chapter about astrology in this book because it involves a belief in phenomena which we cannot explain, and it is a belief which is held by a large proportion of the general public. (P.S. We cannot think of any movies about astrology, unless you count *Scorpio Men on Prozac*, though we are not recommending you rush out to see it.)

These are some of the more commonly reported types of unusual and paranormal experiences and beliefs which remain unexplained at the present time. However, all of these phenomena have in fact been subjected to scientific investigation, and we will be looking at the findings of this research in the forthcoming chapters of this book. Each of the phenomena listed above will be dealt with in a separate chapter.

There is an additional chapter about "Religious beliefs", as these resemble paranormal beliefs in certain respects, mainly in that they are based on personal experience and faith rather than upon scientific evidence. There is therefore a possibility that we can shed some light on the nature of religious beliefs by comparing them with other types of faith-based beliefs such as belief in the paranormal.

The final chapter of the book is entitled "Explaining paranormal beliefs", and here we attempt to provide an overview of what we currently know about paranormal beliefs and offer a few possible explanations of why people believe in the paranormal. In particular, we will be looking at some of the psychological factors which may help to explain such beliefs.

BELIEF IN THE PARANORMAL

Although we live in the age of science, belief in the paranormal remains surprisingly widespread among the general public. Recent surveys in Britain have reported that about 50% of the population believe in extra-sensory perception, 40% believe in ghosts, 22% believe in astrology, and 20% believe that people have been contacted by aliens. Surveys in the United States have reported similar figures for belief in ESP and ghosts, but about 30% believe in astrology, and no less than 36% of Americans believe that people have been contacted or abducted by aliens from distant planets.

As belief in the paranormal is so widespread, it would obviously be helpful if scientists could establish whether or not these phenomena are valid, and whether people are right to believe in them. For some people, an interest in the paranormal is little more than harmless fun, and if you read your stars in the morning newspaper that does not mean that you will take it seriously or allow it to affect your life in any way. But many people do take paranormal events seriously, and some actually make important decisions on the basis of their paranormal beliefs. Some people choose their marriage partner or their job on the advice of an astrologer, while others may decide to move house in order to escape from a ghost or poltergeist. Some people take drastic actions as a result of information they believe they have gained by telepathy, or from a message allegedly conveyed from the spirit world by a medium. Beliefs about paranormal phenomena can also lead to fear and anxiety, as for example with people who live in fear of ghosts and demons, or who are worried about being abducted by aliens.

There may be other less obvious consequences of paranormal beliefs, as for example when people blame their own failures and misjudgements on paranormal influences. After an accident or disaster has occurred, it is sometimes tempting to blame the influence of some unknown force. Some people will conclude that a disaster was "fated" by the stars, or that it was brought about by demons or ghosts of the vengeful dead. This kind of explanation can sometimes provide a convenient excuse for refusing to accept our own responsibility for bad outcomes. This is important, because if we fail to accept our responsibility for our failures, then we will not learn from our mistakes.

TESTING THE VALIDITY OF PARANORMAL PHENOMENA

One obvious reason for studying paranormal phenomena is to find out whether they are actually real. Since many people make important life decisions on the basis of their belief in the paranormal, it is important to find out whether these beliefs are valid. Moreover, if phenomena such as telepathy, clairvoyance, and astrology can be shown to be genuine, then they might offer the potential to enrich our lives. However, if it turns out that these phenomena are not genuine, then they can cause us to make poor decisions and to misunderstand many of our experiences in life. If you base your major life decisions on incorrect beliefs, you will probably not be very effective in dealing with the challenges and demands which life places on each of us. This is one very good reason why paranormal phenomena should be subjected to scientific investigation, and much of this book is concerned with the findings of such scientific studies.

UNDERSTANDING BELIEF SYSTEMS

Besides investigating the actual validity of paranormal phenomena, another reason why psychologists are interested in paranormal research is that it can teach us a great deal about the nature of beliefs and why people adhere to them. People often believe strongly in things for which they have no evidence whatsoever, and it would be helpful if we could understand why they show such unshakable faith.

Another interesting aspect of research into paranormal beliefs involves finding out what kind of people are likely to believe in the paranormal. Perhaps a tendency to accept paranormal beliefs might be linked with certain types of personality, thinking style, or previous experiences and upbringing. Again, this is an area which has been extensively researched, and we now know quite a lot about the type of person who is most likely to believe in the paranormal. This research will be examined in the final chapter of this book.

EXPERIMENTAL DESIGN AND PROCEDURES

Another good reason for studying the paranormal is that it can help to improve the way we design and carry out scientific research. Paranormal research offers a particularly difficult challenge to experimenters, because there are so many factors and possible influences which need to be taken into account when designing an experiment of this sort. For example, if you are trying to investigate whether two people can communicate by extra-sensory perception (which is communication by psychic means rather than through the known senses), then you need to make sure that the people you are testing cannot somehow communicate via any of the normal senses. Information could easily be passed from one person to another by apparently insignificant responses like smiling, coughing, or blinking, which could go completely unnoticed by the experimenter. Such responses could occur quite unconsciously and without any deliberate intention to cheat. But even if the two participants (the "sender" and the "receiver") are kept in entirely separate rooms or buildings, there is still a risk that the experimenters themselves might unwittingly provide feedback at a similarly unconscious level.

Psychologists who wish to investigate paranormal phenomena must design their experiments to control for such possibilities, including many possible factors which are not at all obvious. So, before we accept that the findings of an experiment indicate the occurrence of paranormal effects, we should first ask ourselves what other factors could possibly have produced the effect.

The precautions required for the design of a paranormal experiment can be extremely challenging and require much ingenuity. But by addressing these challenges, paranormal researchers have developed techniques which have helped to improve research design, not just within the paranormal field but also in other fields of psychological research.

One crucial feature of the scientific approach is that it should be possible for other researchers to replicate the findings of any scientific experiment. However, many studies which have been carried out in the past and published in leading scientific journals have proved to be impossible to replicate, and this is particularly true of research on paranormal phenomena. Unfortunately, the replication problem is made worse by the fact that the editors of scientific journals are usually keen to publish exciting new findings (such as claimed evidence for ESP) but are less keen to publish subsequent studies which fail to replicate these findings. This can lead to a publication bias, where positive findings are published and negative findings are not. Psychologists are now aware of this problem, and they are trying to find ways of overcoming it. One the best solutions to the problem of selective publication involves setting up online stores of research findings which include all of the studies carried out on a given topic, including unpublished studies and failures to replicate previous findings. Such records are kept in a store that is accessible to researchers and academics, who are thus able to draw conclusions based on a full review of all of the available studies rather than just the ones which find their way into a journal.

SUMMARY – WHY SHOULD WE STUDY PARANORMAL PHENOMENA?

As explained above, there are three main reasons why it is valuable to study paranormal phenomena. First, we need to find out whether these phenomena are valid, so that we know whether they really occur or not. Second, by studying the kinds of people who believe in paranormal phenomena, we can learn a great deal about the nature of belief, and the reasons why some people acquire and maintain beliefs for which they have no supporting evidence. And third, studies of the paranormal provide a very strict test of the effectiveness of experimental design and may help psychologists to improve their research techniques. Investigations of paranormal phenomena can therefore provide us with some important insights into not only those phenomena but also the nature of human belief systems and how best to study them. Such investigations provide the subject matter of the rest of this book.

2

ASTROLOGY

David Groome

ASTROLOGY AND ITS POPULARITY

Do you ever read your horoscope in the newspaper? A lot of people do. In fact, about 70% of people in the UK read their horoscope regularly. Of course, not all of them take it seriously, but recent surveys have found that 20% of British people and 29% of Americans believe that astrology is true, and that it can tell us something useful about people and their lives. There are many countries where belief in astrology is even more widespread. For example, in India astrology is accepted by most people, and more than 60% of Indians have actually consulted an astrologer.

Astrology is regarded by many people as just harmless fun, but people who take astrology seriously will often make major decisions about their lives on the basis of astrological advice, such as who they should marry or what profession they should take up. So, for many people, astrology is a serious matter which has a very real impact on their lives and on the decisions they make. Even if you are not one of those people, you could still find your life being affected by astrology, since other people may make decisions about you on the basis of your birth date. In a number of countries, it is common for employers to make use of astrologers to help them in the selection of staff, so you could find yourself being rejected for a job because you were born under the wrong star sign.

Since astrology is quite widely accepted and is often used as a method of classifying people and predicting their behaviour, psychologists have become interested in finding out whether there is any truth in astrology and whether it is useful or not. If astrologers are genuinely able to provide insights into the character and future behaviour of individuals simply from their birth date, then psychologists would obviously want to make use of this approach. On the other hand, if astrology does not offer any valid information, then it would be wrong and in fact quite unacceptable to use it in real-life situations such as employee selection or decision making. For this reason, psychologists have seen a need to investigate whether or not the claims made by astrologers are valid.

THE ORIGINS AND RATIONALE OF ASTROLOGY

Astrology has been around for thousands of years, and it was practised in the ancient Egyptian, Greek, and Roman societies. The people of those early times placed great importance on cyclic events such as the passing of the seasons, because they had a profound effect on peoples' lives, on their crops, and indeed on their very survival. Since the stars and planets were found to move in regular cycles, they were assumed to be related to events on earth. In those early times, most things were assumed to be controlled by the gods, and since the stars were thought to be some sort of visible manifestation of the gods, it seemed reasonable to suppose that they might influence a person's destiny, especially those stars which were overhead at the moment of birth.

Over the last few centuries, astronomers have discovered the true physical nature of the stars and their movements, and as a result we no longer regard the stars and constellations as representing gods. Astrologers responded to these new findings by suggesting alternative explanations, suggesting for example that the stars might exert an influence by their gravitational pull. However, this theory also lacks plausibility since it has been shown that the gravitational forces exerted on the earth by the distant stars and planets are very small, so that a new-born baby would actually be subjected to greater magnetic forces from nearby objects such as their cot or the midwife.

One of the biggest problems for astrological theory is explaining why the moment of birth should hold such crucial significance. Thousands of years ago, the moment of birth may have seemed to be a defining moment, because it is observable and appears to be the moment when life actually begins. Today we know that it is merely a point in the gestation period, whose timing is made all the more arbitrary by the possibility of premature or even induced birth.

Nobody has been able to provide a completely plausible explanation for the theory that the position of the stars at the moment of birth should influence our character or our destiny. However, while this may weaken the credibility of astrology, it does not completely disprove it. There are many valid phenomena for which we do not yet have an explanation, and it would be unwise to dismiss them all on that basis. While astrology lacks a plausible scientific rationale, astrologers claim that it has been found to work for thousands of years, and it remains possible that they could be right. The rest of this chapter will be concerned with evaluating the research carried out by psychologists to test out the claims made for astrology. First, however, it would be helpful to consider what astrologers do actually claim.

THE BASIC PRINCIPLES OF ASTROLOGY

Astrologers claim that a person's character and destiny are affected by the stars, and in particular by the position of the stars at the moment of their birth. This influence is believed to be both powerful and lasting, so the stars above you at the moment you are born are thought to shape the kind of personality you will have for the rest of your life, and everything that will happen to you in the future.

The best-known form of astrology, and the one that will be most familiar for those who read their horoscope in the newspaper, divides people's birth dates into the 12 signs of the zodiac, which are 12 bands (or "houses") through which the sun passes during the course of a year. A person's zodiac sign therefore indicates the position of the sun at the moment when they were born, for which reason these 12 signs are also known as "sun signs". This means, for example, that if you are born when the sun is in the house of Pisces, then astrologers would predict that your personality will always tend to show Piscean qualities. You probably already know your own sun sign, but if not (or if you want to look up someone else's sign), the list below provides the generally accepted birth dates for each sign.

THE 12 SUN SIGNS AND THEIR ASSOCIATED BIRTH DATES

1	**ARIES**	21 March–20 April
2	**TAURUS**	21 April–21 May
3	**GEMINI**	23 May–21 June
4	**CANCER**	22 June–23 July
5	**LEO**	24 July–23 Aug
6	**VIRGO**	24 Aug–23 Sept
7	**LIBRA**	24 Sept–23 Oct
8	**SCORPIO**	24 Oct–22 Nov
9	**SAGITTARIUS**	23 Nov–21 Dec
10	**CAPRICORN**	22 Dec–20 Jan
11	**AQUARIUS**	21 Jan–19 Feb
12	**PISCES**	20 Feb–20 March

The 12 sun signs can be divided into four main groups, which are as follows:

Fire signs   (Aries, Leo, Sagittarius)
Earth signs (Taurus, Virgo, Capricorn)
Air signs   (Gemini, Libra, Aquarius)
Water signs (Cancer, Scorpio, Pisces)

People born under fire signs are considered by astrologers to be fiery by nature, tending to be energetic, optimistic, enthusiastic, and aggressive. Those born under earth signs are said to be down-to-earth types, being practical, dependable, logical, and cautious. People born under air signs are considered to be light-hearted, friendly, open-minded, and changeable. Finally, those born under water signs are thought to be imaginative, artistic, sensitive, and emotional.

Astrologers describe fire signs and air signs as the "active" signs, whereas the earth and water signs are "passive" signs. The active signs are said to be characterised by energetic, impulsive, and outgoing tendencies, whereas the passive signs are more restrained, cautious, and withdrawn. These descriptions bear some resemblance to the more scientifically based distinction between "extravert" and "introvert" personality types, a dichotomy which is of some interest to psychologists because it is measurable and thus open to scientific testing (see next section for the findings).

The broad groupings of active/passive signs and earth/water/fire/air signs are regarded as offering only a very general indication of personality; for a more detailed analysis of the individual each sun sign must be considered separately, as they are each considered to have their own more specific qualities. The characteristics usually attributed by astrologers to the 12 sun signs are summarised in the list below.

THE MAIN CHARACTERISTICS ASSOCIATED WITH THE 12 SUN SIGNS

ARIES	Assertive, extravert, energetic, courageous, impulsive.
TAURUS	Reliable, practical, materialistic, persistent, sensitive.
GEMINI	Versatile, lively, witty, articulate, changeable.
CANCER	Sensitive, sentimental, emotional, affectionate, shy.
LEO	Confident, proud, friendly, outgoing, courageous.
VIRGO	Analytical, conscientious, perfectionist, critical, quiet.
LIBRA	Fair-minded, indecisive, imaginative, outgoing.
SCORPIO	Emotional, strong-willed, courageous, reserved.
SAGITTARIUS	Optimistic, impulsive, outspoken, inquisitive.
CAPRICORN	Cautious, practical, logical, reliable, reserved.
AQUARIUS	Open-minded, imaginative, creative, outgoing.
PISCES	Creative, artistic, intuitive, sensitive, shy.

The list above is only intended as a brief summary of the main qualities attributed to the 12 sun signs, and it is not intended to be a complete account of astrology. The sun sign descriptions listed here actually represent a combination of the views of a number of astrologers, but different astrologers are not always in complete agreement about the exact qualities associated with each sun sign. Some astrologers are actually rather dismissive of the sun sign approach and insist that precise details of not only the date of birth but also the exact time and place of birth are essential for the construction of an accurate astrological chart which reflects all planetary influences. However, it is the 12 sun signs which provide the basis for the astrological predictions which appear in magazines and newspapers and which are read by members of the public.

At this point, you might find it interesting to consider the birth signs of some well-known people, and you might like to decide whether they fit the descriptions given above for their particular birth signs. Astrologers would also predict that the people listed under each birth sign should resemble one another in character, so you may wish to check whether this is true for the people on this list.

BIRTH SIGNS OF SOME FAMOUS PEOPLE

ARIES	Eddie Murphy	Victoria Beckham	Vincent Van Gogh
TAURUS	George Clooney	Adolf Hitler	Florence Nightingale
GEMINI	Bob Dylan	Donald Trump	Morgan Freeman
CANCER	Nelson Mandela	Mike Tyson	Will Ferrell
LEO	Barack Obama	Benito Mussolini	Meghan Markle
VIRGO	Hugh Grant	Bernie Sanders	Ivan the Terrible

LIBRA	John Lennon	Mahatma Gandhi	Vladimir Putin
SCORPIO	Hillary Clinton	Prince Charles	Charles Manson
SAGITTARIUS	Winston Churchill	Tina Turner	Woody Allen
CAPRICORN	Michelle Obama	Al Capone	Muhammad Ali
AQUARIUS	Bob Marley	Ronald Reagan	Paris Hilton
PISCES	Albert Einstein	Johnny Cash	Harvey Weinstein

Well, did you come to the conclusion that the astrologers have got it right for the famous people listed here? If so, then you should have found some similarities between the three people listed under each birth sign, and they should match up with the personality descriptions listed in the previous table. Personally, I am not convinced, but I don't want to sway your judgement on this matter. But regardless of what conclusions you have reached so far, it is time to look at what the scientific studies tell us. Can astrologers really do what they claim they can do? Perhaps we should start by considering what astrologers actually claim they can tell us from their knowledge of the stars.

THE CLAIMS MADE FOR ASTROLOGY

Astrologers claim that they can tell us many things from an analysis of our date of birth. Some of the main claims made for astrology are listed below:

1 Astrology can predict our personality and aptitudes
2 Astrology can tell us which professions we are best suited to
3 Astrology can help us to choose the most suitable marriage partner
4 Astrology can predict future events

These are very ambitious claims, and all of them are testable. If astrologers claim to be able to predict these things, then it must be possible to find out whether their predictions turn out to be correct. In recent years, psychologists have carried out many scientific investigations to test the claims made for astrology, and these studies will now be reviewed in detail. Can astrologers really live up to their claims? You will find the answer below.

ASTROLOGY AND PERSONALITY

One of the main claims made by astrologers is that they can predict an individual's personality characteristics from the time and place of their birth. Psychologists have tested these claims by using personality tests to find out whether people born under different birth signs do in fact differ in personality, and whether their personality characteristics are consistent with those predicted by astrologers. There are a number of ways we can test personality, but psychologists have found that questionnaires are often the most accurate measure because they are objective, and they do not involve making any subjective judgements about other people. Using a standard set of questions and a standard scoring system means that each person will get the same score regardless of who administers the test.

A questionnaire study was carried out in 1978 by a professional astrologer called Jeff Mayo together with colleagues, including psychologist Hans Eysenck. A total of 2,324 participants all completed the Eysenck Personality Inventory (EPI), which is a widely used questionnaire measuring both extraversion and emotionality. The birth dates of the participants were then used to sort them into the 12 signs of the zodiac, in order to find out if there were any personality differences between one birth sign and another. The hypothesis put forward by Mayo was that the "active" signs (i.e. fire and air) would be more extraverted than the "passive" signs (i.e. earth and water). Remarkably, this is exactly what was found in this study, though admittedly the differences between adjacent signs were fairly small.

These findings appeared to offer some support for astrology at first, but a different explanation was subsequently found for the findings of

Mayo's study. The participants in their experiment all knew quite a lot about astrology, and they were all well aware of what characteristics were supposed to be associated with their own sun sign according to astrologers. A person who knows that their birth sign is characterised by extraversion may come to believe that they are more extraverted than they really are, because that would fit in with their expectations and beliefs. If their knowledge of astrology suggests that they should be an extravert, then they are more likely to see themselves as extraverted, and this will affect the answers they give on a questionnaire.

Evidence was soon obtained to confirm that this was indeed the correct explanation for the Mayo data. Hans Eysenck and David Nias carried out a similar study in 1982, which revealed that the differences in extraversion scores between different sun signs completely disappeared when the study was repeated on people who had no knowledge of astrology. Clearly, then, the effect had been caused by the knowledge and expectations of the people tested in the Mayo study. Many subsequent studies have confirmed that there are no measurable differences between the personality test scores of people born under different signs of the zodiac, except when the people being tested have a good knowledge of astrology and know what sort of personality is expected for each birth sign.

These questionnaire studies offer no support for astrology, but they do tell us something important about human beings. They demonstrate that people can be influenced by their prior knowledge and expectations, which can significantly affect the way they see themselves. This is an important finding, with implications for many fields of psychological research. It also offers a valuable message for everyone: the way that people see themselves is significantly influenced by their previous knowledge and beliefs.

ASTROLOGICAL BIRTH CHARTS AND PERSONALITY

An interesting study was carried out in 1985 by Shawn Carlson, who actually brought in a number of professional astrologers to help with their experiment. Each astrologer was asked to predict the likely personality characteristics of a participant by constructing a birth chart from their birth details alone (i.e. date, time, and place of birth), but without actually meeting the participant. The same participant also completed a personality questionnaire known as the CPI (California Personality Inventory). The astrologer was then asked to choose which one from a choice of three different peoples' CPI scores showed the best match with their own astrological prediction of personality. The three CPI profiles included the correct one (i.e. the CPI scores obtained from the participant for whom birth details had been provided), together with CPI profiles for two other people chosen at random. Carlson found that the astrologers were unable to match up their astrological assessment with the corresponding CPI scores beyond chance level. Moreover, it was found that the participants themselves were unable to recognise their own astrological personality profile as produced by the astrologer, again from a choice of three.

Carlson's study is important because it tested the ability of professional astrologers to predict personality from birth information. It turned out that they could not, and in fact they were unable to provide any information about personality using astrological techniques.

ASTROLOGICAL TIME TWINS

"Time twins" are people who are born at the same time on the same day. They are not "twins" in the normal sense, as they are not actually biological relatives and therefore have no genetic similarity. This makes time twins a very suitable target for study, since astrology would predict that they would grow up to be very similar people with a similar destiny. However, scientific studies have shown that time twins are not usually very similar to one another at all. For example, in 2003 Geoffrey Dean and Ivan Kelly tested no fewer than 1,400 time twins, measuring over 100 variables relating to personality, abilities, life events, and behaviour. They found no correlations between the scores of time twins on any of these measures. Since all of their pairs of time twins were born within five minutes of one another in the same location (London), astrology would predict strong similarities, but none were found.

ASTROLOGY AND PROFESSION

Astrologers are often called in to give career advice to their clients, and in some countries, astrologers are actually employed to help with personnel selection. The claim that astrology can predict suitability for a particular occupation is therefore a matter of great practical importance. It is thus a claim which needs to be tested.

One criterion of career success is the achievement of excellence and fame in one's chosen occupation. This was the criterion chosen by French psychologist Michel Gauquelin (1972), who looked up the birth dates of 16,000 famous people to find out whether fame and success in a particular field was associated with any particular sun sign. Astrologers have suggested, for example, that Scorpios and Leos tend to make good soldiers, Sagittarians make good lawyers, and Capricorns make good politicians. In fact, Gauquelin found no support for any of these predictions, nor was there any significant link between birth sign and success in any particular profession.

However, Gauquelin did find something of interest in his results. When he looked at the actual time of day when famous people tended to be born, he discovered that there were apparently some slight variations from a chance distribution. Famous sportsmen and soldiers were more likely to have been born at two particular periods of the day, which roughly corresponded to the times when the planet Mars was on the rise. There were similar, albeit smaller, effects for a few other professions.

Gauquelin's findings were seized upon by astrologers as proof that the stars really could influence success in a particular field, but this claim was quite unjustified. In the first place, the variations from the expected random distribution of birth times reported by Gauquelin were very small, and in any case they were not consistent with the predictions made by astrologers. The findings therefore offered no support whatsoever for sun sign astrology, as Gauquelin himself admitted. Another big problem for Gauquelin was that subsequent studies failed to replicate his findings, and some evidence was found that he had omitted certain celebrities from the study whose data did not support the Mars effect. In 1991, Michel Gauquelin destroyed all of his research files and committed suicide.

A study carried out by British statistician Alan Smithers in 1984 took a different approach. Instead of focusing on famous people, Smithers investigated the relationship between birth sign and profession for a sample of ordinary people from the general population. This made it possible to test a very large population sample, and in fact Smithers obtained his data from the 1971 UK population census, from which he obtained the birth dates and occupations of more than two million British adults. Smithers counted up the total number of people born under each of the 12 sun signs for each of the 27 different occupations in which the people in his sample had chosen to work.

The distribution of birth signs for the various professional groups caused some surprise at first, because some birth signs did actually occur far more frequently than others for a given profession. These intriguing results raised the question of whether or not the varying sun sign peaks might be the result of astrological influence. In order to answer this question, Smithers recruited a team of 15 professional astrologers, who were asked to predict the sun sign which they felt was most likely to predominate in each of the 27 main professions represented in the survey. Unfortunately, the astrologers were unable to agree on their predicted sun sign for most of these professions, and in fact there were only ten of the 27 professions for which they could reach any consensus. The birth signs they chose for each of these ten professions were as follows:

SUN SIGNS PREDICTED BY ASTROLOGERS FOR TEN OCCUPATIONS

1. Author/Journalist **Gemini**
2. Baker **Taurus**
3. Car mechanic **Aries**
4. Civil engineer **Capricorn**
5. Clerk/Cashier **Virgo**
6. Coal miner **Scorpio**

7	Hairdresser	**Libra**
8	Optician	**Virgo**
9	Secretary/Typist	**Virgo**
10	Tailor/Dressmaker	**Libra**

Smithers compared these predictions with the actual peak birth dates obtained from the census data for each of the ten professions, and he found that the astrologers had only guessed the correct sun sign in one profession out of the ten. For the profession "Authors and Journalists" the astrologers had predicted that Geminis would predominate, and this was indeed the most frequently occurring sign. However, for the other nine professions, the most frequently occurring birth sign was not the one suggested by the astrologers. For example, the astrologers had predicted that most secretaries would be Virgos, but the census data showed that secretaries were most likely to be born under Cancer, and Virgo was actually the least frequently occurring sign for this profession.

A success rate of one correct "hit" out of ten guesses was roughly what would be expected by chance, so there was no evidence that the astrologers had achieved anything better than a random guess. Smithers concluded that his data offered no support whatsoever for sun sign astrology. Smithers did concede that those employed in a particular profession may not always be the people most suited to it, because many people do not get much choice about which occupation they take up. However, if astrological forces really did exert significant control over peoples' aptitudes, then we would expect some effect to show through in their choice of occupation, but no such effect was found.

Although Smithers' data offered no support for conventional astrology, an explanation was still required for the predominance of certain birth signs in some professions. In fact, it turned out that there was a surprisingly simple explanation. When Smithers examined seasonal birth trends in the UK population, some large variations were found between different social/educational groups which clearly explained the seasonal variations in his data. He found that for manual workers the birth rate peaks in late autumn, whereas for non-manual workers the peak birth rate occurs in the spring. These seasonal trends were found to explain all of the sun sign variations in Smithers' data.

Smithers found no evidence in his data to support astrology, but as with many other studies it did provide some valuable insights into the factors which can influence research findings. His study demonstrates how easily a variation from the norm can be attributed to the stars when in fact it merely reflects some general social trend. One important point that we can learn from this study is that we should never attribute data variations to astrological influences without first considering all of the other possible causes.

ASTROLOGY AND MARRIAGE COMPATIBILITY

Astrologers claim that some sun signs are particularly compatible with one another, and that choosing a marriage partner from the right sun sign will increase the chances of a long and happy marriage. For example, Virgos and Capricorns are said to be a good combination, with excellent marriage prospects. However, this is another claim that has not stood up to scientific testing. In 2007, David Voas published a study based on data from the 2001 UK census, which examined the marriages of no fewer than ten million married couples, probably the largest sample ever tested in a study of astrology.

From a survey of the birth dates of the ten million couples, Voas reported that those who shared what astrologers considered to be "compatible" birth sign pairings were no more likely to enjoy a lasting marriage than those with an "incompatible" pairing. Voas also found that marriages between couples with "compatible" birth signs did not occur any more frequently than those between "incompatible" signs, which suggests that people are not disproportionately attracted to potential partners with sun signs which are compatible with their own. So, it can be concluded that sun sign combinations do not predict whether people will make successful marriage partners, nor do they predict whether people will be attracted to one another.

PREDICTING FUTURE EVENTS BY ASTROLOGY

One of the most ambitious claims made by astrologers is that they can predict future events from studying the stars. Their view is that the stars determine the basic conditions which favour a particular outcome, so that although that outcome is not absolutely inevitable, it is highly probable. This rather cautious approach allows them a convenient way out in case their predictions fail to come true. Basically, this version of astrological prediction is a bit like predicting that there will be more people wearing overcoats next winter than there were in summer. This prediction is not completely certain to come true, but if it doesn't then a lot of people will be cold and shivering.

In the past, some astrologers have succeeded in predicting future events, and these successes have been widely publicised. However, one important reason why astrologers often appear to get their predictions right is that their correct predictions attract public attention, whereas their incorrect predictions tend to be disregarded. For example, an American astrologer called Jean Dixon became famous in the 1960s for correctly predicting that President Kennedy would die young. However, most people forgot that Jean Dixon had made three predictions at that time. The first was that Kennedy would meet an early death (which he did). Her second prediction was that Russians would reach the moon before the Americans (which they didn't). Her third prediction was that World War III would begin in 1958 (again, not as far as I recall, but perhaps I was not paying attention). Many people were impressed that she had predicted Kennedy's death, but her unsuccessful predictions went largely unnoticed.

Several studies have been carried out to investigate the accuracy of predictions made by astrologers, but they have all found that such predictions rarely came true apart from the occasional lucky guess. And on those rare occasions when a prediction did come true, it usually involved an outcome that was very likely to happen anyway, or was expressed in such vague terms that it would be difficult to decide whether it came true or not. For example, in 1979 Culver and Ianna examined the predictions made by a number of professional astrologers for the coming year. Altogether three thousand separate predictions were submitted, but less than 2% of them actually came true. Furthermore, the few that did come true were the most likely ones and were often expressed in extremely vague terms. For example, two of the most successful predictions were "Tension will continue in the Middle East" and "There will be a tragedy in the Eastern USA next spring". It would be a reckless person indeed who would choose to bet money against either of these events occurring, that year or any other year.

CONCLUSIONS

From the studies reviewed above, it is clear that astrologers are unable to predict future events, career aptitude, marriage compatibility, or personality, with anything beyond a chance level of accuracy. It would therefore be unwise to base any important decisions on astrological predictions, and it would be unacceptable for astrologers to play any part in tasks such as personnel selection, career advice, or selection of a marriage partner.

While it is fair to say that no evidence has been found in support of astrology, this is not quite the same as saying that astrology has been totally disproved, since the existence of astrology is essentially non-falsifiable. It is not possible to prove that something does not exist or that it is never true, and this applies to astrology just as it does to other unsupported claims such as those for Santa Claus or the unicorn. Despite the lack of any supporting evidence, there will always remain a faint possibility that there are some valid astrological effects. However, what we can say for certain is that any such effects are so small that they cannot be detected by any known method of testing, so they can probably be safely ignored for all practical purposes.

Given that there is no scientific evidence for astrology, it seems strange that so many people are prepared to believe in it. This kind of irrational belief is actually quite an interesting finding in its own right, and it is more interesting to psychologists nowadays than the question of whether astrology is true. Many studies have been carried out which help shed some light on such beliefs. For example, a study by Snyder and Schenkel in 1975 found that most people accepted an "astrological" description of their personality as being very accurate, despite the fact that everyone received the same description, regardless of their birth sign.

This experiment made use of the "Barnum Effect", named after the famous showman who claimed that people will believe anything about themselves so long as it includes "a little something for everybody". The trick is to say things which are as vague and generalised as possible, things which virtually anyone could identify with. It is also a good idea to make the description positive and flattering, in other words telling people what they want to hear. For example, if you tell someone "there are some people who do not fully realise your good qualities", most people would probably agree that this applies to them personally. If you are not convinced that this strategy works, try reading through the stars column of your daily newspaper. If you try hard enough you will find some snippets that apply to you in every one of the 12 zodiac signs.

One possible reason why the guidance of astrologers is accepted so uncritically is that most people are keen to get a better understanding of themselves and others. The rather limited insights offered by psychologists are just not good enough for those who seek a quick and easy method of predicting the behaviour of the people they meet. Such individuals will often accept a system such as astrology which promises to give them the insights they are looking for.

Our final conclusion to this chapter is that the available scientific evidence offers no support at all for astrology. This being the case, it would be unwise for anyone to use astrology for making decisions about important aspects of their lives. On the other hand, there is probably no harm in reading your stars in the newspaper if you want to. And you may even find that it sometimes comes true.

3

EXTRA-SENSORY PERCEPTION

Michael Eysenck and David Groome

EXTRA-SENSORY PERCEPTION

In this chapter, our main focus will be on extra-sensory perception (ESP). This term is used to refer to various mysterious phenomena such as telepathy (where information is received from another person without use of any of the known senses) and precognition (where information is somehow detected from the future). These phenomena appear to be inexplicable (and impossible!) in terms of our knowledge of physics and psychology.

Approximately 50% of British and American citizens believe in ESP, but in contrast most scientists dismiss ESP as totally implausible and unscientific. The great majority of psychologists are highly sceptical about the existence of ESP, and they argue that demonstrating the existence of ESP requires higher standards of evidence than most other phenomena in psychology. As the British psychologist Richard Wiseman explained, "If I said that there is a red car outside my house, you would probably believe me. But if I said that a UFO [unidentified flying object] had just landed, you'd probably want a lot more evidence". We agree with Richard. However, as scientists we also believe that even unlikely phenomena such as ESP deserve to be investigated thoroughly.

The history of research on ESP goes back almost a hundred years. In what follows, we will chart this history with an emphasis on the interesting characters strongly for or against the existence of ESP.

EARLY HISTORY

The person who put ESP research 'on the map' was an American botanist, Dr Joseph Rhine (1895–1980). He first became interested in the paranormal in 1922 when attending a talk by Sir Arthur Conan Doyle (the creator of Sherlock Holmes). Doyle argued there was strong scientific evidence for life after death, and Rhine became intrigued by the notion that science could potentially resolve such issues, and other controversies concerning paranormal phenomena.

In 1927, Joseph Rhine moved to Duke University in Durham, North Carolina. What he then did made him famous. He decided to replace murky approaches to the paranormal such as séances, Ouija boards, and so on with a truly scientific approach. He did this with the assistance of his colleague, Dr Karl Zener, who invented a pack of cards with each card showing a star, a square, a circle, three wavy lines, or a cross. There were 25 cards in the pack, with five cards showing each of the symbols. In a typical experiment, one person (the sender) looked at each card in turn while another person (the receiver) tried to read the sender's mind and wrote down their best guess as to the identity of each card. As there were only five different types of card, the receiver could be expected to guess one card out of every five correctly just by chance. So even assuming that ESP does not take place, receivers would on average be expected to make only about five correct guesses out of the 25 cards (i.e. 20%). Rhine, together with his wife Louisa and several colleagues, carried out a large number of experiments with the Zener cards, and they discovered several individuals whose guessing performance was substantially better than chance expectation, thus providing apparent evidence for ESP. For example, when Hubert Pearce was tested in 1932, he was correct 40% of the time (hugely significant statistically compared to chance expectation of 20%). Overall, Rhine claimed his research produced very strong evidence for ESP.

Can we accept Rhine's findings at face value? The answer must be "no", for three main reasons. First, while Rhine himself was probably honest, although perhaps rather gullible, several of his co-workers were clearly guilty of fraud. For example, Dr Walter Levy, a trusted colleague of Rhine's, confessed to cheating while carrying out an ESP experiment and was fired from his job. Towards the end of his life, Rhine admitted that four of his experimenters had been caught red-handed engaging in dishonest research behaviour.

Second, while Rhine claimed to have adopted a scientific approach, his experiments contained numerous methodological flaws. For example, Hubert Pearce was often allowed to shuffle and cut the Zener cards himself, and participants would sometimes help with the checking of their responses against the actual order of the cards. In addition, according to Terence Hines:

> The methods the Rhines used to prevent subjects from gaining hints and clues as to the design on the cards were far from adequate. In many experiments, the cards were displayed face up, but hidden behind a small wooden shield. Several ways of obtaining information about the design on the card remain even in the presence of the shield. For instance, the subject may be able sometimes to see the design on the face-up card reflected in the agent's glasses. Even if the agent isn't wearing glasses it is possible to see the reflection in his cornea.

Third, several other researchers failed to replicate Rhine's key findings. Although most attempts to replicate the Rhines' findings failed to find any evidence of ESP, there was one exception: Dr Samuel Soal (1889–1975), a mathematician at Queen Mary College. Soal used a variant of Rhine's approach with each of five animal pictures presented on five cards within a 25-card deck. He discovered two people (Basil Shackleton and Gloria Stewart) who performed amazingly well when guessing which animal was shown on each card. Alas, we cannot accept these findings at face value. Betty Marwick, a member of the Society for Psychical Research, found some of Soal's target sequences (i.e. the order in which cards were to be presented) had additional numbers written in to them afterwards. All of these additional numbers corresponded to hits, which suggests that they were fraudulent. When these numbers were omitted, the remaining findings were at chance level. Soal reacted to such criticism in a somewhat paranoid fashion. In fact, those who worked with Soal regarded him as a remarkably introverted and secretive person, and one colleague worked with him for several years before discovering he was married!

In sum, there was general disenchantment with research on ESP around 35 years ago. As Scott Lilienfeld has pointed out, this research was characterised by "a consistent inconsistency". In addition, it lacked "a crucial feature that is a hallmark of mature laboratory sciences, namely a readily transportable 'experimental recipe' that can yield replicable results across independent laboratories". As we are about to see, this pessimistic state of affairs appeared to change dramatically in 1994.

GANZFELD *EXPERIMENTS: EARLY RESEARCH*

The disappointments associated with the experimental approach to testing ESP pioneered by Joseph Rhine led researchers to look for something better. The most influential of these newer approaches was introduced by an American parapsychologist called Chuck Honorton (1946–1992). His key assumption was that individuals are most likely to exhibit ESP if they are in a relaxed state undistracted by input from their visual and auditory senses. This basic idea goes back to the *Yoga Sutras* of Patanjali written approximately 3,500 years ago. In this work, it is suggested that ESP powers are present when someone is in a state of deep meditation known as *samadhi*. More prosaically, if we assume the mental information that can allegedly be detected by some individuals is extremely weak, we need a procedure that minimises extraneous noise and thereby maximises the probability that the very weak ESP signal can be detected, essentially by increasing the signal/noise ratio.

In 1974, Honorton devised the *ganzfeld* (whole field) procedure based on the above assumptions. The receiver lies comfortably on a bed with halved ping-pong balls over their eyes, while soothing noise resembling the sound of the sea is presented via headphones. When the receiver is relaxed, the sender looks at a picture or video clip for several minutes and the receiver tries to use ESP to obtain information about it. Finally, the receiver is shown the target picture plus (typically) three others, and tries to select the correct one.

There are several differences between Honorton's *ganzfeld* procedure and Rhine's earlier card-guessing approach. Of potential importance, Rhine adopted a 'forced-choice' approach in which participants were required to guess the target from a limited set of symbols. In contrast, the *ganzfeld* involves a 'free-response' approach in which the range of possible targets is almost limitless. It is argued that the flexibility of the latter approach increases the probability of detecting ESP.

Early *ganzfeld* studies appeared to produce promising evidence of ESP. However, various criticisms were made of these studies concerning the possible influence of the experimenters, so in 1983 Honorton embarked on *Autoganzfeld* studies involving computer control of most aspects of the experimental procedures. In Honorton's experiments, the receiver and sender were placed in different rooms, both of which were soundproofed. These rooms were separated from another room in which the experimenter sat. A video clip was presented repeatedly to the sender over a period of 30 minutes and the receiver said out loud what they were thinking. Then the receiver tried to select the target video clip from a choice of four items (the target item plus three distractor items). Chance performance would therefore be 25%, but performance very significantly higher than that was sometimes obtained in this experimental set-up.

During the 30-minute sending period, the sender and the experimenter can both hear what the receiver is saying. During the judging process, the experimenter reminds the receiver of what they said during the preceding sending period. In the prompting condition, the experimenter also points out potential similarities between what the receiver had said and each of the four video clips in turn. A crucial part of the entire procedure is that there is only one-way communication into the receiver's room so that they cannot communicate with the sender or experimenter through any of the normal sensory channels.

Findings using the *ganzfeld* and *Autoganzfeld* procedures have been very variable, and failures of replicability make it very hard to come to any clear conclusions. One approach that sounds like a possible solution is to carry out a "meta-analysis", in which we combine all the relevant findings from many different research studies on a particular topic (in this case *ganzfeld studies*) so that we can obtain an overall perspective on what has (or has not) been discovered. Since all the findings are analysed statistically, it appears on the surface that meta-analysis provides a very effective and relatively objective approach that should avoid the biases and distortions present in some individual studies. Honorton carried out various meta-analyses on *ganzfeld* and *Autoganzfeld* research. Here we will focus on his last such meta-analysis (reported in 1994 with Daryl Bem as co-author). It was claimed in this meta-analysis (published in *Psychological Bulletin*, one of the most prestigious journals in psychology) that *ganzfeld* and *Autoganzfeld* experiments provided very strong evidence for the existence of ESP. Overall, participants correctly guessed the identity of the target on approximately 35% of trials, whereas only 25% would be expected from chance guessing. Bem and Honorton regarded these results as strong evidence for the existence of ESP. They also reported several other interesting findings using their meta-analytic approach. For example, they found that individuals showing the strongest evidence of ESP tended to be artistically creative, had previous ESP-like experiences, and had previously studied a mental discipline such as meditation.

GANZFELD *EXPERIMENTS: PROBLEMS*

Many people were hugely impressed by Bem and Honorton's research. They seemed to have discovered a strong ESP effect when combining findings from numerous studies in different parts of the world. Alas, all is not as it seems! There are various problems with Bem and Honorton's approach. First of all, of the 28 studies included in Bem and Honorton's meta-analysis, no fewer than nine of them came from

Carl Sargent's laboratory at Cambridge University. Curiously (or perhaps not so curiously, as we will see), it is not mentioned anywhere in the article that one-third of the experiments came from this one laboratory.

Why are we making all this fuss about Sargent's experiments? The answer lies in the detective work of a British psychologist Susan Blackmore. She spent many years in the early part of her career involved in ESP research as a firm believer in its existence. However, her findings were consistently non-significant and she became progressively more sceptical of the ESP research of other researchers. Susan Blackmore paid a fateful visit to Carl Sargent's laboratory in 1979 in an attempt to find out why his findings were so much more impressive than her own. Blackmore discovered several suspicious errors and biases in the conduct of Sargent's experiments. Most damagingly, when Blackmore asked Sargent to provide his full data so that apparent irregularities could be examined closely, he refused to do so. As a consequence, a committee of the Parapsychological Association asked Sargent in 1984 to provide his raw data, but again he refused their request. This lack of cooperation clearly suggests that Sargent had something to hide.

A second problem with the *ganzfeld* studies is that there are several kinds of evidence suggesting the experimenter had a substantial impact on the results. For example, there was much more evidence of ESP when the experimenter provided prompts than when they provided none. More strikingly, the hit rate when a target video clip was presented for the first time in the experiment was only 14% but for later occurrences the hit rate rose to 44%. We might imagine that this could have reflected a practice effect, with the receivers becoming more sensitive to ESP information over time. However, that cannot be the case because the great majority of receivers took part in only a single trial. Any practice effect would have to involve the experimenter, since each experimenter was in charge of over 40 trials on average.

Third, there were several methodological inadequacies in at least some of the studies, some of which were highlighted by the British psychologist Richard Wiseman, whose name we mentioned earlier. Richard was a stage magician before becoming a psychologist, and he is a well-known ESP sceptic. He discovered that there is some disagreement and confusion about what actually happened in most of the early *ganzfeld* experiments. For example, in the 1993 conference proceedings of the Parapsychological Association, it states with respect to those studies that senders "were encouraged to be vocally supportive when they heard mentation [thinking] that was on target". A very different version of events was given to Richard Wiseman when he contacted researchers involved in *ganzfeld* studies. Three of them believed any trial was aborted if the experimenter heard any noises coming from the sender's room. What is certain is that no attempt was made to monitor or record the sender's voice at any point. As a consequence, the extent to which senders spoke or made non-verbal noises is unknown.

Fourth, in 1999, Julie Milton and Richard Wiseman reported a meta-analysis of 30 *ganzfeld* studies from seven laboratories, and their findings were very different from those reported by Bem and Honorton. They reported that "the new *ganzfeld* studies show a near-zero effect size and a statistically non-significant overall cumulation".

GANZFELD *EXPERIMENTS: PROGRESS?*

Yet another meta-analysis on ESP was reported in 2010 by Lance Storm, Patrizio Tressoldi, and Lorenzo Di Risio. Their meta-analysis was based on 59 studies reported during the period 1997–2008, a time during which many methodological flaws and inadequacies present in earlier research had been eradicated. They compared ESP performance in three types of study: (1) *ganzfeld*; (2) non-*ganzfeld* noise reduction (e.g. meditation); and (3) control (no *ganzfeld* or noise reduction).

What did Storm et al. discover? There was very strong evidence of ESP in the *ganzfeld* studies, moderately strong evidence of ESP in the non-*ganzfeld* noise reduction studies, and no evidence of ESP in the control studies. Storm et al. also addressed the issue of whether selected participants (e.g. meditators, believers in the paranormal, etc.) showed more evidence of ESP than non-selected ones. Of interest, the selected participants only outperformed non-selected ones in the *ganzfeld* condition. Thus, as predicted, easily the strongest ESP effects were obtained among selected individuals exposed to the *ganzfeld* procedure.

These findings are impressive in various ways. First, as mentioned already, the studies included in the meta-analysis were more methodologically sound than previous ones. Second, we have moved on from the simple question "Does ESP exist: yes or no?" to the important question of the factors which determine the magnitude of any ESP effects (e.g. experimental conditions; individual characteristics).

The results sound convincing enough, but you can probably guess what we are going to say next! Problems with Storm et al.'s meta-analytic review were rapidly identified. Jeffrey Rouder and colleagues highlighted two problems: (1) there may have been difficulties with randomising the order of targets in studies using manual rather than computerised randomisation; and (2) the meta-analysis omitted unpublished studies, most of which showed little or no evidence of ESP. This latter point suggests that there is a problem of "selective publication", whereby non-significant findings are much less likely to be published than significant ones. For example, a survey indicated that 70% of significant ESP studies conducted at the University of Edinburgh were published compared to only 15% of non-significant ones. When Rouder et al. re-analysed the Storm et al. data including the ignored unpublished studies but omitting studies using manual randomisation, the findings changed dramatically. Storm et al.'s analysis favoured the existence of ESP by a factor of 6 billion to 1, but this figure shrank to about 300 to 1 in Rouder et al.'s re-analysis!

In spite of the popularity of meta-analyses, they provide a less 'objective' view of scientific knowledge than you might imagine. Suppose you are a fervent believer in ESP and have decided to carry out a meta-analysis on *ganzfeld* studies. You must first decide on the inclusion criteria – which studies should be included in your meta-analysis? There is perhaps a natural tendency to select your inclusion criteria to ensure that studies strongly supporting ESP are included whereas those obtaining non-significant findings are excluded. You might also decide to analyse the data in numerous different ways and then focus on those analyses apparently providing the strongest evidence for ESP. So, the decisions made by those carrying out a meta-analysis may be influenced by confirmation bias, which means seeking evidence that supports one's beliefs while ignoring evidence which does not.

INDIVIDUAL DIFFERENCES IN ESP PERFORMANCE

Researchers have found that some people seem to better than others at producing a convincing score on an ESP test. Several studies have suggested that high ESP scores are easier to obtain when the people being tested are creative and imaginative individuals. It has also been reported that the best ESP scores are produced by individuals who are able to achieve a very deep state of relaxation, and who are able to open their senses to accept any kind of perceptual input in a passive and uncritical manner, without indulging in any form of judgment or analysis.

Some people are better at achieving such states than others, and consistent differences have been found between individuals in qualities such as the tendency to analyse input extensively. Analytical processing can therefore be seen as a characteristic personality trait of a particular individual, and it seems to be a trait which makes that individual a bad choice of participant if you are trying to demonstrate the occurrence of ESP. These individual differences, which distinguish good participants from bad participants, have helped researchers to recruit the most promising people to include in their tests of ESP. But these same individual differences have also been found to favour other types of performance, such as the capacity for subliminal perception. This will be considered further in the next section.

ESP AND SUBLIMINAL PERCEPTION

Research carried out by cognitive psychologists has established that we can sometimes register and retain information from a perceptual input even though it has not reached our conscious awareness. This phenomenon of perception without awareness is known as "subliminal perception". One way in which it has been demonstrated is by flashing a word or picture on a screen for a tiny fraction of a second, so that its exposure is too brief for the observer to perceive consciously. However, although the observer fails to notice this image at a conscious level, it can still influence their perception of subsequent input, so evidently it must have registered at some unconscious level. For example, if the word "sad" is flashed very briefly on the screen, followed by a picture of a human face without any obvious expression, the face is more likely to be described as sad even though the word sad was not consciously perceived.

A number of researchers have pointed out that there are some similarities between subliminal perception and ESP. For example, both subliminal perception and ESP involve the perception of a very weak signal which may not reach full conscious awareness. Also, both of these phenomena occur most readily when the participant is in a state of extreme relaxation and is prepared to receive any perceptual input without thought, judgement, or analysis of any kind.

Caroline Watt has recently suggested that ESP may involve the same mechanism as that involved in processing subliminal perception, so that an ESP input is initially registered without reaching conscious awareness. However, as with subliminal perception, this unconsciously perceived input may subsequently impinge on consciousness and can affect conscious thoughts and emotions. Some support for this hypothesis comes from the finding that individuals who are very defensive in their response to subliminal inputs of a stressful or threatening nature are also less likely to score highly on a test of ESP. Watt considers that this finding offers some support for a link between ESP and subliminal perception, and it also suggests that ESP might be at least partly processed by normal cognitive mechanisms.

It must be emphasised that none of this research on the relationship between ESP and subliminal perception provides any clear confirmation that ESP actually occurs. Indeed, the claim that there are similarities between ESP and subliminal perception, and a possible link between their underlying mechanisms, appears to rest on an assumption that ESP is a valid phenomenon. This is an assumption which is certainly open to debate. However, even if ESP does not turn out to be a true and valid phenomenon, it is possible that a person's ability to somehow simulate ESP might still be related to their capacity for subliminal perception. For example, a person who has enhanced sensitivity to subliminal perception might be able to use that sensitivity to detect very subtle subliminal signals via the five normal senses, which can assist them in improving their score on an ESP test. And this might enable them to achieve scores which seem to show the occurrence of ESP even though no actual ESP has occurred.

CONCLUSIONS AND FUTURE DIRECTIONS

Research on ESP has had a chequered history. Every apparent step forward seems to be followed by a step backward. However, there are some signs of progress. First, there has been a steady improvement in the methodological rigour of experimentation in ESP. This is an essential prerequisite for the task of establishing the validity of ESP. Second, there is an increasing recognition that, while meta-analysis is potentially valuable, it is subject to important limitations because of the possibility of biased selection of studies and confirmation bias. Third, the research of Storm et al. represents an important attempt to identify the situational and individual factors influencing the strength of any ESP effect. Fourth, researchers are beginning to focus on the size of the ESP effect rather than simply its statistical significance. A limitation with the use of statistical significance testing is that a very small ESP effect (e.g. 27% hits vs. chance prediction of 25%) would still produce a highly significant result if the data involves thousands of trials. But in reality, the effect would be too small to be of any importance.

What about the future? First, we need to enhance the meta-analytic approach. Watt and Kennedy (2017) proposed changes to greatly reduce confirmation bias. There should be pre-registration of studies, so that for example those planning to carry out a meta-analysis should document all key details of their meta-analysis (e.g. rationale; hypotheses; methods of data analysis) *before* embarking on the meta-analysis itself. In addition, there should be total openness or transparency so that everyone can see precisely which decisions were made by the researcher designing the meta-analysis. It is noteworthy that Watt and Kennedy introduced a pre-registration for meta-analytic studies in ESP as long ago as 2012.

Second, instead of assuming that any claimed ESP effect must either be entirely due to ESP or entirely due to methodological inadequacies, it should possibly be accepted that ESP findings might reflect a combination of both factors. In 2016, Dick Bierman and colleagues proposed an interesting method for disentangling these two factors. They carried out computer simulations to assess the likely impact of various questionable research practices on findings based on meta-analyses of *ganzfeld* experiments. Their conclusion was that the size of the ESP effect in such meta-analyses was probably inflated by questionable research practices. However, there was also evidence for a genuine (but very small) ESP effect.

Third, it would be useful if all researchers registered their experiments on ESP *prior* to embarking on the experiment. This would serve the valuable function of making it easier for meta-analysts and others to take account of *all* ESP research in their analyses. The importance of this is that, as indicated earlier, unpublished studies are much more likely than published ones to involve non-significant findings. If unpublished studies are ignored, this can seriously distort our understanding of the empirical evidence.

In conclusion, we have to accept that for the time being we cannot say with absolute certainty whether ESP exists or not. As we have explained in this chapter, there is some research which appears to support ESP, but there is other research which does not, and there are some possible reasons why the research supporting ESP may not be entirely convincing. One thing that we can say with reasonable certainty is that even if ESP does exist, then it must be a fairly weak effect, because it seems to exert very little influence over anything in our real everyday lives. For example, if ESP were a real and powerful phenomenon, you would expect that it would by now have been used for some practical purpose such as detecting crime or winning lots of money in a casino. But the police have found that psychics cannot help them, and the casinos continue to make a profit. So as far as ESP is concerned, the jury is still out. But, somewhat ironically, nobody knows when the jury will come back in, or what verdict they will deliver. To know that, you would need to be psychic.

4

SPIRITS AND MEDIUMS

David Groome and Robin Law

COMMUNICATING WITH SPIRITS

A medium is someone who claims that they can communicate with the spirits of dead people and pass on messages from the spirit to a living person (known as the "sitter") during a séance. The sitter is usually a relative or friend of the deceased person, and they will obviously be very keen to be in touch with the person they have lost.

A growing number of mediums have become television stars in recent years, and you may have seen some of them. The American medium John Edward can be seen contacting the dead on a regular basis on American and British TV, and so can Tyler Henry, the self-styled "Hollywood medium", who specialises in contacting the deceased relatives of movie stars. In Britain things are not quite so glitzy, with the more down-to-earth approach of television mediums such as Sally Morgan, or "Psychic Sally", as she is better known. And who can forget the immortal Doris Stokes? Actually, Doris seems to be quite literally immortal, as she continues to dabble with mediumship despite the fact that she herself passed on to the spirit world some years ago.

Throughout history, people in various different parts of the world have tried to contact the dead, and even in biblical times there were people who claimed to be in touch with their dead ancestors. For example, King Saul in the Old Testament managed to get some useful advice and information from the reincarnated spirit of Samuel (see: the Book of Samuel). Elsewhere in the Bible (Leviticus), it is noted that God actually disapproves of mediums who try to distract the dead from their heavenly duties, which makes it all the more surprising that Doris Stokes has been welcomed into the Kingdom of Heaven, but apparently she has.

Mediums became particularly popular in the West following the rise of the Spiritualist Church in the late nineteenth century. Even today mediums continue to thrive, and a recent survey showed that about 25% of the UK population has consulted a medium or psychic at some time in an effort to contact deceased relatives and friends. But is there any actual evidence that any of these claims of mediumship are valid? In fact, there have been plenty of scientific investigations of such mediums, and in this chapter, we will examine what they found.

THE MYSTERIOUS FOX SISTERS

The first case of alleged mediumship to be investigated and widely publicised involved two American sisters called Kate and Margarita Fox, who first came to the attention of the public in 1848. At that time the Fox sisters were still children, living in a small town near to New York called Hydesville. The Fox sisters claimed that they heard banging noises which they believed to be communications from the spirit of a man who had died and been buried beneath their house, and they devised a way in which he could answer their questions using two raps for a "yes" and no raps for a "no". Using this system, the Fox family were able to come up with plenty of information about the supposed spirit, including the claim that he had been murdered. This caught the interest of many people from the surrounding areas, and a large number of them began to attend séances with the sisters in order to observe their efforts to contact the spirit. Once they had heard the alleged spirit's rapping and clicking noises for themselves, most of the observers became convinced that the noises they heard were indeed emanating from some disembodied soul since they could find no other explanation.

Others who attended the séances were more sceptical, however, and some suggested that the girls were making the noises themselves. Many years later, the Fox sisters admitted that they had in fact been cheating, and they even demonstrated the way in which they had created the mysterious rapping sounds by clicking their joints. Although they later retracted their confession, it seems fairly likely that they had indeed faked the whole thing in an effort to gain attention and fame. However, although the Fox sisters had confessed to being frauds, their confession seems to have gone largely unnoticed by those who believed in mediumship, and by this time many new mediums had emerged who claimed to be in contact with the dead.

THE DAVENPORT BROTHERS AND THEIR BAND OF CELESTIAL MUSICIANS

In 1864, two American brothers, William and Ira Davenport, performed what they claimed was a demonstration of the activities of spirits. Their performance involved the two brothers both being tied up and left in a large cabinet, which also contained various musical instruments such as bells and tambourines. Shortly after the doors of the cabinet were closed, observers were astounded to hear the sounds of bells and tambourines being played. It was generally accepted by those present in the audience that this could only be the work of spirits called up by the brothers, since everyone had seen the boys being tied up at the start, and they were seen to be still tied up when the cabinet doors were finally opened again.

While there were many who regarded the Davenport brothers' performance as a convincing demonstration of the presence of spirits of the departed, others were not so sure. A few cynical types even wondered if the brothers had somehow been able to untie their bonds, play the instruments, and then tie themselves up again before the cabinet doors were opened to reveal them in their bound and helpless state. Two well-known magicians of the period, Harry Houdini and John Mullholland, were among the doubters. Houdini showed that he could produce the same performance as the Davenports by using straightforward trickery. Mullholland discovered that the Davenports had several confederates in the audience who were secretly assisting with the mysterious sound effects. He also described one of their performances in which they produced music while being allegedly tied up, but using darkness rather than a cabinet to conceal their activities. When the stage was suddenly illuminated in mid-performance by some rather mischievous member of the audience, the Davenports were revealed to be not only free of their bonds but actually holding the tambourines and bells. Indeed, this was for them the final bell.

MRS PIPER BAFFLES EVERYONE

Although many of the early mediums failed to stand up to serious scrutiny, this did not rule out the possibility that others might be genuine, and there were a number of mediums who managed to convince those who investigated them that they were not fakes. One such was an American woman called Mrs Piper, who was investigated in 1896 by William James, one of the most eminent psychologists of the period. William James reported that his investigations of Mrs Piper's communications with the spirit world had been entirely convincing. He described how she had contacted a spirit who had been able to provide detailed personal information about the people present at her séances, even though these individuals were apparently complete strangers to her. Even more impressively, Mrs Piper was able to correctly identify those people who had met her spirit guide during his lifetime and those who had not. Of course, it would have been possible to obtain this kind of information by straightforward detective work, but there was no evidence that Mrs Piper ever carried out such enquiries.

The late nineteenth century was in many ways the golden age of mediums, and there was much public interest in the claims made by these individuals. As a result of the séances held by the Fox sisters and others who claimed to be able to contact the spirits of the dead, the Spiritualist movement came into being and it soon attracted millions of followers, all of whom were keen to contact their deceased friends and family members once again. But as Spiritualism and mediums grew in popularity, scientists also began to take an interest in their supposed abilities and in testing the validity of their claims. During this period, an organisation was set up in Britain called the Society for Psychical Research (SPR), the aim of which was to carry out scientific investigations of paranormal phenomena such as mediumship.

An SPR member called Richard Hodgson was actually sent to America to carry our scientific tests on Mrs Piper, and he investigated her psychic capabilities with great enthusiasm and with some considerable ingenuity. He was careful to provide her with a supply of complete strangers as the sitters at her séances, and he took care to keep their true identity a secret from her. He even commissioned a private detective to follow her secretly, but he found no evidence to suggest that she had tried to collect information about possible séance attenders. Despite Hodgson's best efforts, he was unable to find any evidence that Mrs Piper was cheating in any way.

EUSAPIA PALLADINO TAKES ON THE SOCIETY FOR PSYCHICAL RESEARCH

While Mrs Piper had managed to convince her investigators, most mediums of the period did not stand up so well to scientific scrutiny. One of the most famous and successful mediums of that time (the 1890s) was an Italian woman called Eusapia Palladino. She had impressed observers by demonstrating a variety of unexplained noises and items of furniture moving for no apparent reason, and she claimed that these mysterious events were the work of the spirits of the dead. However, when her claims were investigated by members of the Society for Psychical Research in 1895, she was caught cheating. This led to much debate and controversy among the members of the Society. While the discovery of an act of deception might reasonably be seen to cast doubt on all of Palladino's previous claims, there were still many among her supporters who took the rather generous view that although she had cheated on one occasion, this did not necessarily prove that she had cheated on all of the other occasions. This response in itself demonstrates an interesting aspect of human behaviour, which is that true believers in a phenomenon are not easily persuaded to change their views, even in the face of clear evidence that they are wrong. However, those who continued to believe in Palladino's psychic powers were a small minority, and most people regarded her as a fraud. It is worthy of note that the Society for Psychical Research concluded at around this time that even after investigating mediums for more than half a century they had found no convincing evidence that mediums were genuinely able to contact the dead.

PROFESSIONAL CONJURERS AND STAGE MAGICIANS

One important reason for casting further doubt on the claims of mediums is the fact that conjurors and stage magicians have been able to duplicate their performances using simple deception and conjuring tricks, with absolutely no pretence of possessing psychic powers of any kind. In fact, Richard Hodgson (the Society for Psychical Research investigator mentioned earlier) carried out such a demonstration as early as 1887, when he invited members of the public to attend a fake séance during which he used trickery to create an apparent dialogue with spirits. Most of his sitters found his demonstrations of mediumship completely convincing, and in fact they showed a surprising inability to think of possible ways in which the same effects could be achieved by deception.

Over the years, a number of professional stage magicians have demonstrated that they can perform the same feats as the self-proclaimed psychics and mediums by using their conjuring skills rather than employing any psychic powers. James Randi is a very successful stage magician who has performed for many years on stage and TV as "the Amazing Randi". He is also the bane of all who fraudulently claim to possess psychic powers, and he has devoted much of his life to unmasking them. Randi has demonstrated that he can use his conjuring skills to perform exactly the same procedures (such as spoonbending and guessing the contents of a sealed envelope) as alleged psychics such as Yuri Geller. However, Randi is happy to admit that he is using trickery and conjuring skills, and he argues that those who claim to be using psychic powers to create these illusions are cheats who are deliberately deceiving the public. For more than 20 years, James Randi offered to pay the sum of one million dollars to anyone who could convincingly demonstrate the use of psychic powers under controlled laboratory conditions and under close observation by psychologists and skilled magicians. Many people have taken up Randi's challenge, but so far none of them have succeeded in winning the money.

MRS PUTT TAKES UP THE MAGICIAN'S CHALLENGE

One of the many people who tried to win James Randi's million-dollar prize was a British medium called Patricia Putt. Mrs Putt is a professional medium who has appeared on television on several occasions. She claimed to be able to channel information from a deceased Egyptian called Ankhara, who was apparently able to provide her with information from other spirits which her clients had generally found to be highly accurate. Her powers of mediumship were tested in 2008 by two leading British researchers, Richard Wiseman and Chris French. They arranged for Patricia to meet ten people, one at a time, all of whom were strangers to her. In order to prevent any possibility of Mrs Putt gaining information directly from the sitters, they were each required to cover themselves with a cape and a balaclava, and they were not permitted to speak.

As each of the ten sitters were brought into the room, Mrs Putt was asked to try to find contacts in the spirit world who could provide personal information about these individuals. Mrs Putt's readings for each of the ten people were written down, and each of the sitters were given the ten transcripts and was asked to pick out the one which most applied to them. It seems reasonable to assume that if Patricia Putt had succeeded in coming up with true and accurate personal information, such as a description of a friend or some personal experience from the past, then this information would have been recognisable to the extent that all ten of the sitters should have been able to pick out their own reading. In fact, none of the ten sitters was able to correctly identify their own reading. This was not a good result for Mrs Putt, as you would expect to get at least one correct match out of ten just by chance. Wiseman and French concluded that Patricia Putt had not succeeded in demonstrating any evidence of mediumship or psychic powers of any kind, though they did accept that she was not guilty of deliberate fraud, as she apparently believed that her psychic powers were genuine and was quite perplexed by her own failure to demonstrate them.

THE MEDIUMS VS. THE SCIENTISTS

More recently, Richard Wiseman and his colleague Ciaran O'Keeffe have carried out carefully designed investigations of five other self-proclaimed mediums. As with the Patricia Putt study, no evidence was found for any genuine mediumship powers, and once again the sitters found nothing in the readings given to them which they particularly recognised from their own lives or personal experiences.

The studies carried out by Richard Wiseman and other psychologists who study mediumship are far more scientifically designed and more carefully controlled than was the case for the early mediumship investigations. In the early days, for example the study of the Fox sisters mentioned earlier, the investigator would simply turn up at a séance to observe what he or she was allowed to observe. But, crucially, the séance was arranged and controlled by the medium, who was the main person in charge of the proceedings. Communication between the medium and their sitter would take place freely, and there would be ample opportunities for the medium to obtain information and to make deductions from what their sitter said. The medium was also able to observe the appearance and clothing of the sitter, which could provide further clues. For example, do they have rough hands that are used to manual work? Are they wearing a wedding ring? Such observations could obviously provide the medium with a few shreds of information which they could use as a starting point for further probing and questioning of the sitter.

In more recent years, Richard Wiseman and other investigators have devised testing procedures which eliminate most of these possible sources of information by preventing the medium from seeing or hearing the sitter or observing the sitter's responses to any suggestions made to them by the medium. Great care is taken to ensure that no information can be passed directly from the sitter to the medium, or from the experimenter to the medium. Perhaps the biggest change in the investigation techniques now used, in contrast to those employed in earlier studies, is that the experimenter now has compete control over the setting and the procedure, rather than allowing the medium to be in charge of everything. It is interesting to note that as the design of the testing procedure has become more rigorous, the performance of the mediums under test has generally become less convincing.

SUGGESTION AND TRICKERY CAN EASILY CONVINCE PEOPLE

Richard Wiseman has demonstrated that many people can be easily convinced that they have witnessed genuine communication with the spirit world, even if the effects they experienced were created by a mixture of conjuring tricks and suggestion. Wiseman is in fact an accomplished conjuror, and in his earlier life he had actually performed as a stage magician. A man who can produce the flags of all nations from your left ear will clearly have no difficulty in making a table move without any detectable input of his own. Wiseman and his colleagues carried out an experiment in 2003 involving a fake séance, during which various objects were made to move by trickery. However, most of the sitters were unable to explain the movements they had witnessed, and some concluded that psychic phenomena must have been involved. Wiseman was also able to demonstrate that sitters could be easily convinced that an object had moved even if it had remained stationary. All that was needed was a suggestion from the séance leader that the object was moving, and the other people in the group would begin to see the movement, too. Those who came to the séance with a prior belief in psychic phenomena were far more susceptible to these suggestions than were the non-believers, probably because they were actually expecting to see such things even before they arrived.

COLD READING

James Randi has also described the techniques used by magicians to acquire information about a member of the audience by using a method known as "cold reading". Cold reading makes use of subtle clues given out by the chosen audience member which enable the performer to make reasonably good guesses about that person' character, their concerns, and their life. Of course, the guesses will not always be correct, but they don't need to be, as the chosen person (often someone recently bereaved) will probably be so keen to believe what they are being told that they will convince themselves of its accuracy.

The first principle of cold reading is to prepare the sitter, making it clear to them that any message that the reader can obtain from the spirit world will contain information intended personally for the sitter rather than for the reader, so the sitter will therefore need to make an effort to interpret what they are being told. The reader will explain that as they are only acting as a channel for the message, and as the message is not intended for them, they will probably be unable to explain all of it in any precise way to the sitter. The sitter is thus primed to expect fairly vague and possibly confusing information which they must try to make sense of in terms of their own life and experience.

A second principle of cold reading is that the reader will always keep their messages rather vague and general, and as far as possible the content of the message will be something that will actually apply in some way to almost anyone. For example, "the deceased person was fairly elderly, and they have suffered some misfortunes in recent years". Well, who doesn't have a friend or relative who could fit that description? Skilled readers will have acquired a good knowledge of the kind of statement which will be particularly likely to ring true for a sitter who falls into a certain age group, or a particular social or educational sub-group of the population. Careful observation of the sitter, their appearance, their conversation, and their manner can help the reader to guess which groups the sitter is likely to fall into.

Another useful cold-reading technique is for the reader to employ a "fishing" strategy, by saying things to the sitter which may trick them into giving away something specific about their lives. For example, "I am getting a message about a person who may have been involved in some trouble or difficulties early in their life" is a statement which contains no definite information but may lead the sitter to identify someone they have known who fits this very general description.

Cold-reading techniques have been used extensively by stage performers, and they seem to be employed by self-proclaimed psychics and mediums, too. However, this does not necessarily mean that all psychics and mediums are frauds, or that they are deliberately setting out to deceive and trick people. The majority of them are probably perfectly honest people who genuinely believe that they possess some psychic power, and they may well be making use of cold-reading techniques without even realising that they are doing so.

CONCLUSIONS

As there does not seem to be any convincing evidence that mediums really can contact the spirits of the departed, we need to look for other possible explanations of their claimed ability to do so. We have already seen that stage magicians such as James Randi and Richard Wiseman are quite capable of producing the same kinds of performance and stage effects as those produced by a medium, but by using conjuring skills and cold reading instead of psychic powers. This demonstrates what can be achieved by a skilled conjuror, and it clearly offers a plausible explanation of the performances achieved by mediums.

Late last night I sat down to watch the TV for a few minutes with my cup of cocoa, and who should be on TV but Tyler Henry, the very charming Hollywood medium and "psychic to the stars". I watched him with much fascination as he proceeded to apply every known technique of cold-reading, but it was all done quite skilfully, and as far as I could tell, quite sincerely, too. At one point he mentioned to his sitter that her deceased friend had been very much concerned about health matters for the period immediately preceding his death. The sitter was amazed at this startling and apparently accurate revelation. I was amazed, too, but possibly for a different reason.

5

ALIEN ENCOUNTERS AND ABDUCTIONS

David Groome and Robin Law

THE ABDUCTION OF BARNEY AND BETTY HILL

In the autumn of 1961, an American couple called Barney and Betty Hill were driving home towards their house in New Hampshire late in the evening. Barney was a postal worker and his wife Betty was a social worker, both in their early 40s, and they were returning from a vacation trip to Niagara Falls. As darkness closed in around them on a long empty stretch of road, they spotted a bright light in the night sky which seemed to be moving about in a strange way. They stopped the car and got out to take a closer look with a pair of binoculars, and from its jerky movements and flashing coloured lights on its surface Barney and Betty realised that this mysterious flying object was not an aircraft, nor was it a falling star. In fact, it was not like anything they had ever seen before, which raised the possibility that it was some kind of UFO (Unidentified Flying Object), which some people believe are spacecraft visiting us from a far-off galaxy. When the Hills returned to their car and attempted to drive on, the bright object suddenly flew towards them at considerable speed and stopped abruptly in front of them. Barney described it as resembling a huge pancake, about 60 feet across. He would later describe how several figures emerged from the craft, and although they were shaped rather like humans, they were smaller and greyish in colour. Barney and Betty then noticed a loud buzzing sound and a feeling of strange vibrations going through their bodies, and they felt themselves descending into a trance state where they were only faintly aware of what was happening.

When they returned to full consciousness, they were back in their car, unsure of what had happened to them, but a glance at their watches revealed that more than two hours had passed since they had last been fully conscious. By this time, Barney and Betty were wondering whether they could have been abducted by aliens, and this appeared to be confirmed for them by their subsequent attempts to remember exactly what had taken place. A few days after their abduction experience, Betty began to have dreams in which she recalled the events of the abduction in detail. In her dreams, the Hills were taken on board the spacecraft by the little grey men, where they were placed on tables so that they could be examined. Many physical tests were carried out, especially concerning their eyes, ears, mouths, and genitals. They were also questioned, and they discovered somewhat remarkably that the aliens were able to communicate in English, though they also used another language of their own to talk among themselves.

Two years after this incident, the Hills agreed to undergo hypnosis in an effort to find out more about what had happened to them. This was carried out by a hypnotist called Benjamin Simon. Under hypnosis, both Barney and Betty were able to produce a detailed account of their abduction, and they both described events which showed a close similarity to Betty's dreams. By this time, Barney and Betty Hill had become entirely convinced that they had been the victims of an alien abduction. The Hills' case was the first claim of alien abduction to be widely publicised, but it would not be the last.

ALIEN ABDUCTIONS GO MAINSTREAM

The Hills' alien abduction claims were widely publicised during the next few years, and their story attracted great interest throughout

America. There were many magazine articles about the incident, which became known as "the Hill abduction" since many people accepted the claim that the Hills had genuinely been abducted by aliens. In 1966, a writer called John G. Fuller wrote a book about the Hill's alien encounter, entitled *The Interrupted Journey*. The book was a great success and sold in large numbers, and in 1975 it was made into a TV movie called *The UFO Incident*. There would subsequently be a number of major films about alien encounters of this kind, such as *Close Encounters of the Third Kind*, *ET the Extra-Terrestrial*, and a popular TV series called *The X-files*. You have probably seen some of these films and TV shows, and I hope you enjoyed them. But for some people, these productions were not seen as fiction, and many believed that they depicted real events. Certainly the movies and TV shows created a far wider awareness of the nature of alien encounter claims, and they established a standard alien abduction format which provided the inspiration for a host of subsequent claims.

In the years that followed, many more people would report that they too had been abducted by aliens. Often their accounts bore close similarity to those of the Hills, with descriptions of similar events and the same little grey men. In 1975, a forestry worker in Arizona called Travis Walton claimed to have been abducted by aliens whose appearance and activities bore a close resemblance to those reported by the Hills. It is perhaps not entirely coincidental that Walton made his claim just two weeks after the Hills' abduction movie, *The UFO Incident*, had been shown on television. However, as with the Hills, Travis Walton's claim brought him considerable fame and financial rewards, too. He wrote a successful book about his abduction entitled *Fire in the Sky*, which was subsequently turned into a film. Another early abduction claimant, a Mississippi sharecropper called Riley Martin, was actually given his own radio show. And then there was Whitley Streiber, who happened to be a professional writer and novelist. His writing career was not going too well until 1985, when he reported that he too had been the victim of an alien abduction. Again, the result was a successful book, entitled *Communion*, and a lucrative film script soon followed.

It seems that we do not need to look far to find a possible motivation for making an abduction claim, though that is not to say that the individuals involved were necessarily making up their abduction stories. Some may have genuinely believed that they had been abducted, but irrespective of the truthfulness of their claims, it is clear that many stood to gain public acclaim and sometimes money, too.

In the years that followed these early reports, claims of alien encounters would really take off, even if the flying saucers may not have done. It has been reported that over the last 50 years, nearly four million Americans have claimed to have been abducted by aliens, which amounts to about 2% of the entire US population. If these claims are all true, then the aliens must be working flat out to keep up with demand. A cynic might think that the average alien would have more important things to spend their time on.

WHY SHOULD ALIENS WANT TO ABDUCT PEOPLE?

Various different theories have been proposed in an effort to explain why aliens would want to cross the vastness of the universe in order to abduct randomly chosen people who were just minding their own business. One theory suggests that the aliens wish to know more about us, and that all of their testing and examining of human bodies is motivated by a desire to find out what stage of evolution has been reached by the earthlings, and whether they are ready to be contacted or even perhaps used for some unknown purpose. Some abductees claimed to have had devices implanted in their bodies which could be monitored from some distant planet. But no such device has ever been found, and when a claimant has been able to identify such an implant, it has invariably turned out to be something of distinctly earthly origin such as a pacemaker or a dental filling.

Another popular theory is that the aliens wish to mate with humans in order to create a new hybrid race, possibly to overcome some genetic weakness in their own alien stock, or to create immunity against some disease or threat which is currently wiping out the beleaguered inhabitants of some distant star. The theory that aliens wish to breed with us mainly arose from the fact that many abductees claimed to have been persuaded to have sex with the aliens who abducted them, and a number of female abductees have even claimed that they were made pregnant by their alien captors. However, this theory loses some credibility from the fact that none of these women actually gave birth to an alien/human hybrid, despite the fact that this would normally have been the expected outcome in such cases. Most of these allegedly pregnant abductees turned out to be not pregnant after all, and those who did give birth produced normal human babies, often bearing an uncanny resemblance to a friend's husband or a man they happened to have met at work. This is just hypothetical, of course, but you might expect that a woman who has got pregnant by cheating on her husband needs to come up with a convincing excuse. A story about being abducted by aliens in flying saucers might seem like a long shot, but it could be worth a try if nothing else comes to mind.

One further question mark hovers over the theory that aliens are trying to investigate our higher functions or possibly interbreed with us. If the aliens are really trying to harvest our superior genes or measure our capabilities, then why do they choose to abduct farm labourers, lumberjacks, and the occasional postal worker? Why do they not set their sights on the great thinkers of our society, or alternatively perhaps our elected leaders? Why, for example, have they not chosen to abduct Donald Trump? Hey, now there's an idea.

SCIENTIFIC RESEARCH ON ALIEN ABDUCTIONS

Unfortunately, it has not been possible to carry out scientific experiments on actual cases of alien abduction, because they always occur at unexpected times and places and there is never a research team ready and waiting there on the spot. This makes it impossible to completely rule out the possibility that alien abductions might occur, because (as Karl Popper has pointed out) it is impossible to prove that something does not exist or never happens. That is why we must in theory keep an open mind on the occurrence of alien abductions, just as we should keep an open mind on the existence of the Yeti, the unicorn, and Father Christmas. But the lack of any positive evidence for these mythical creatures must inevitably lead us to doubt their existence, even if we can never completely rule them out. The same applies to claims of alien encounters and abductions. There is no way that we can prove for certain that they do not ever occur, but we should none the less remain sceptical since we have no convincing evidence that they do.

Despite some four million known claims of alien encounters, not a single claimant has been able to provide any concrete evidence that the encounter genuinely took place. None of these alien encounters were actually witnessed by anyone apart from the claimants themselves. No physical evidence of the encounter remains either, and there are no remnants or souvenirs to be displayed which can stand up to scientific examination. Although many of the alleged abductees claimed to have tracking devices implanted into their bodies, none have proved to be genuine. And none of those claiming to have been inseminated by aliens have actually delivered the alien hybrid baby that they were apparently expecting.

Some believers in alien abduction have argued that the widespread agreement between the various claimants' descriptions of their experiences offers support for the validity of abduction claims. They point out that many of the accounts of abduction show a consistency which seems to confirm a standard procedure being adopted by the alien visitors, as well as showing close agreement in the description of the aliens themselves. However, sceptics point out that the early abduction stories, such as that of the Hills, have been so widely publicised that the similarity of subsequent claims could simply reflect the copying of previous abduction stories.

There is absolutely no hard evidence that any of the four million reported alien encounters actually took place, so most scientists conclude that they probably did not. This suggests that those claiming alien abductions must have been mistaken, and this leads us to ask what might have caused them to make such a mistake. One interesting line of enquiry involves investigating whether there is a particular type of person who is liable to make such claims, and this research will now be examined.

WHAT KIND OF PEOPLE MAKE ALIEN ABDUCTION CLAIMS?

Is there a particular type of person who is likely to make a claim of an alien encounter or abduction? If so then this might go some way towards providing a possible explanation for abduction claims. In fact, abduction claimants do tend to show certain patterns of personality which distinguish them from more typical members of the general population.

A number of studies have indicated that alien abduction claimants tend to score highly on tests of fantasy proneness, which means that they tend to experience very vivid fantasies and have more difficulty than others in distinguishing between fantasy and reality. Not all studies have succeeded in confirming this finding, but bearing in mind that this research mostly involves questioning a person about their tendency to imagine things, it might be expected that abduction claimants would tend to be wary of admitting to living in a fantasy world. The evidence suggests that abduction claimants tend to be very imaginative people, and the things they imagine seem more real to them than for most other people. These findings were summed up in a 2008 research paper by Chris French, who also noted that abduction claimants were more prone to experience hallucinations than the average person, and claimants also reported higher levels of loneliness, unhappiness, and depression. The claimants group also had a higher than average suicide rate, though there was no clear evidence that they had any increased susceptibility to actual psychiatric illness.

Recent research has revealed that people who report having suffered abuse in childhood tend to become more fantasy-prone in later life, and they are also more likely to make alien abduction claims. A possible explanation for these findings is that abuse victims may resort to fantasy as a coping strategy, since their childhood may be so distressing that they need to escape into an imaginary world where they can feel safe. This tendency to indulge in fantasy may predispose abuse victims to create imaginary worlds, possibly including encounters with aliens. However, another possible explanation for this association is that fantasy-prone individuals may be more likely to imagine not only alien encounters but also childhood abuse.

Both of these proposed explanations for the association between abduction claims and fantasy-proneness seem to be fairly plausible. However, a rather more dubious explanation has been put forward by believers in alien abduction, who suggest that aliens are particularly keen to abduct people who are imaginative and fantasy-prone, for some reason that is not entirely clear. So here you have three possible explanations, but the third one does not seem very convincing. However, there is a growing body of evidence that the majority of alien contact or abduction claims are a consequence of fantasy proneness, which may in some cases lead to the creation of false memories.

FALSE MEMORIES

Human memory does not function like a video recorder. Our memories of events are highly flexible, and they decay over time and can be distorted by subsequent experience. Experimental psychologists have shown that even subtle prompts in the phrasing of a question can distort memory for events. In fact, following decades of research, we now know that it is possible to induce false memories for episodes which never actually occurred.

One demonstration of the creation of a false memory was reported in a study by Roediger and McDermot in 1995. Their participants were shown a list of related words such as 'sewing', 'knitting', 'thread', 'pin', and 'injection', but with another strongly associated word missing from the list (e.g. 'needle'). When tested later, participants would often recall that the missing word had actually appeared in the list. However, if you think this kind of thing only happens in laboratory studies, then you might be surprised. Pioneering researchers like Elizabeth Loftus have demonstrated the risks of false memory formation in real-world situations, such as the distortion of memory in eyewitness accounts resulting from cues provided during police questioning.

In a classic 1974 study by Loftus and Palmer, participants viewed footage of a car crash and were later questioned about the crash. During the questioning, some participants were asked how fast they thought the cars were going when they 'hit', 'contacted', or 'bumped' into one another, while others were asked how fast they thought the cars were going when they 'smashed' into each other. Those asked the more emphatically worded questions (e.g. "smashed") were more likely to recall the cars as moving faster. They were also more likely to report seeing broken glass at the scene, though in fact there was none. Since these classic studies, false memory research has strongly influenced modern police interviewing techniques, and it has also shed light on the general fallibility of human memory.

Some studies have been conducted to test whether alien abduction claimants are especially prone to false memories. In one of these studies, using a variant of the false memory task used by Roediger and McDermott (described above), Susan Clancy reported in 2002 that people who claimed to have memories of alien abduction were also more susceptible to false memories, revealed by their increased likelihood of incorrectly recalling the presentation of the missing items on the list. There is some cause for caution here, as a study by Chris French in 2008 failed to find significant differences between the false memory scores of claimants and non-claimants. However, claimants did score higher than non-claimants for factors such as fantasy proneness, the tendency to hallucinate, and paranormal belief. Interestingly, claimants were also more likely to believe they possessed psychic ability. So, it remains uncertain whether abduction claimants are more susceptible to false memories than the general population, but they do seem to be more prone to fantasy and less able to distinguish the products of their own imagination from reality.

As mentioned earlier, researchers have been able to demonstrate that it is possible to induce false memories for whole episodes which never actually occurred. In the first of these studies to explore alien abduction claims, Otgaar and colleagues in 2009 attempted to induce false memories of abduction in a large number of young children, from 7 to 12 years of age. They did this by telling the children that their mothers had reported that the child had been abducted by aliens, and by also showing them a fake newspaper report suggesting that these abductions are extremely common. You may already be wondering whether it is entirely acceptable to implant such false memories in children as part of an experiment, and indeed this study has been heavily criticised as it obviously raises some serious ethical issues. However, the results clearly supported the false memory account of alien abduction claims, as the majority of the children falsely remembered being abducted by aliens. In subsequent interviews, the children often produced additional details of their abduction experience, such as describing the presence of cameras and equipment, the number of people who had been present, and specific details like being transported to the UFO through a beam of blue light.

THERAPY AND HYPNOSIS

The potential risk of psychotherapists inducing false memories in their clients has been a matter of great concern in recent years. This is partly due to the large number of people claiming to have recovered memories of childhood abuse during therapy. Needless to say, memories of abuse are a very serious issue, and cannot be taken lightly. But in some cases, there has been reason to suspect that false memories were being reported, and this has led to a concern that false memories were being created during therapy. Indeed, these risks are now recognised in the guidelines of all major psychological and psychiatric associations.

Some of the ways in which therapists can unintentionally induce false memories in their clients have been described by Elizabeth Loftus. She noted that therapists may suggest a possible explanation for their patient's problems which, due to the therapist's authority and the influence of social pressure, can encourage the client to believe that they remember the suggested causative events. Loftus also noted that therapists will often follow this with probing questions which encourage the patient to further explore a particular line of enquiry and search for memories that fit this account. In some cases, it can become impossible for a client to distinguish these imagined and suggested events from their real memories.

As it happens, many alien abduction claimants had undergone hypnosis which could have influenced their claims. For example, Thomas Bullard carried out a review of reported alien abductions in 1989, and he discovered that hypnosis had been employed in about 70% of cases. It is therefore possible that false memories induced by hypnosis could explain some alien abduction claims. Although hypnosis may not necessarily influence the content of memory in any clear way, it may increase the level of conviction one has of a memory being true.

The possibility of creating false memories of alien abduction through hypnosis was explored by Alvin Lawson. Having some experience of using hypnosis on people who claimed to have been abducted, Lawson had become sceptical of their claims and decided to find out what would happen if he were to hypnotise people who had never claimed to have met aliens. In 1984, Lawson hypnotised eight volunteers with little prior knowledge of alien encounters and asked them to simply imagine that they had been abducted. Lawson was surprised to discover that the accounts they produced were strikingly similar to those of people who had claimed to have been genuinely abducted, right down to the level of small details.

It is tempting to conclude that false memories induced by hypnosis may completely explain most alien abduction claims. However, the explanation does not appear to be that simple. Bullard conducted a more detailed analysis of the accounts presented by Lawson's hypnosis volunteers and noted that despite clear similarities in content, the imagined accounts lacked the lucidity of those of genuine abduction claimants. Bullard suggested that the most plausible explanation would be that the actual abduction claimants had based their accounts on some real experience, not of an actual abduction but of some similar experience which had actually taken place. Subsequent hypnosis might increase the sense of the memory feeling real, but it may not be the initial source of the memory. However, this still leaves the question of why anyone would ever suspect they had been abducted by aliens in the first place, and a possible answer to this is considered in the next section.

SLEEP PARALYSIS

A possible explanation for a claimant's initial suspicion that they have been abducted by aliens arises from a consideration of the time and place that alleged alien encounters tend to occur. As first noted by Spanos and colleagues in 1993, the majority of reported alien encounters occur in the bedroom late at night, and typically involve the victim waking up to discover that aliens are present beside their bed. This is not to suggest that the encounters are merely dreams, and indeed this is not what the evidence suggests.

Spanos and his colleagues pointed out that abduction accounts bear a strong resemblance to a little-known condition called sleep paralysis. Sleep paralysis occurs when a person wakes from sleep but finds that their body remains paralysed for a short period. This can be accompanied by auditory and visual hallucinations, a sensation of pressure on the chest, and the sensation of floating or flying. One of the typical forms of hallucination known to occur during sleep paralysis is that of feeling there is an intruder or presence of some kind in the room, possibly approaching the individual or even sitting on their chest. Psychologists have suggested that this type of hallucination may be brought on by heightened anxiety and vigilance. Clearly, then, sleep paralysis and the associated hallucinations share some things in common with the typical report of alien encounters, but it is not immediately clear why a person would mistake an episode of sleep paralysis for an alien encounter. However, we know that sleep paralysis is a relatively common condition, and around 8% of people experience sleep paralysis at some point in their life, but most of those people have never heard of sleep paralysis and are unaware of its existence. So, an individual experiencing sleep paralysis for the first time will have great difficulty understanding what is happening to them. They will probably seek an explanation for this disturbing experience, and one possible explanation that might occur to them is that they have been visited by aliens.

A further piece of evidence for such a view lies in the historical and cultural differences in people's accounts. There are stories in the folklore of many cultures which involve night-time abductions in which the individual is carried off by some supernatural being. Sometimes the abducted person rises out of their body, and in some stories, they return to their home with some kind of gift or magical power. People's interpretations of these accounts often seem to reflect the cultural framework of the particular time and place they are living in. The most popular interpretations in earlier times were often religious in nature and have therefore tended to include angels, spirits, or demons. In modern Western society, perhaps extra-terrestrial visitors might better fit the popular cultural narrative of our less-religious times. Depictions of alien beings are widespread in films, TV shows, books, and even computer games. An interpretation based on alien abduction might therefore seem plausible to someone seeking to explain away the terrifying experience of sleep paralysis in the modern age.

Can sleep paralysis explain all abduction claims? Probably not. As Susan Blackmore has noted, the characteristics of sleep paralysis are seen in many cases of claimed abduction, but not in every case. However, sleep paralysis would appear to offer a far more reasonable explanation for many of these claims than the idea of extra-terrestrial visitors who are hell-bent on abducting somebody.

CONCLUSIONS

The evidence from several decades of research on alien abductions does not support claims that people are actually being abducted by aliens. However, it does not suggest that all abduction claimants are deliberately lying about their experiences. There is no good evidence to suggest that typical claimants are dishonest, nor that they are psychiatrically impaired. However, what the evidence does suggest is that abduction claimants are more fantasy-prone and more likely to experience hallucinations than the general population, and these tendencies may lead to the creation of false memories which may seem completely real to the individual concerned. In some cases, this might be induced by some well-meaning therapist or hypnotist, and in others, possibly an isolated episode of sleep paralysis. Research continues in this area, and though we do not yet have a definitive explanation for these reports, the alien abduction explanation would appear to be among the least likely of all the possibilities we can think of.

6

RELIGIOUS BELIEFS

Michael Eysenck

One of the few incontrovertible facts about religion is that it is of enormous importance worldwide. A few years ago, a team of American researchers asked individuals in 155 different countries whether religion formed an important part of their daily lives. On the basis of the answers they received, the researchers estimated that 68% of humans (representing approximately 4.6 billion people) regard religion as being of genuine importance to them.

The other side of the coin is that almost one-third of the human race does NOT regard religion as important in their everyday lives. Indeed, it has been estimated that there are over half a billion atheists worldwide. Of all the thousands of religions, that number is exceeded only by the numbers of Christians, Muslims, and Hindus. Atheists are 58 times more numerous than Mormons and there are 41 times as many atheists as Jews.

You may well be wondering why there is a chapter on religion in a book on parapsychology (indeed, we would be surprised if you didn't!). We can explain ourselves by retelling the old story about the psychologist in a strip club who turns his chair around to look at the audience. In similar fashion, we will NOT be focusing directly on religious beliefs and the value of faith. Instead, we will metaphorically be turning our chairs around to study psychological differences between those who espouse a religious faith and those who do not.

We will rarely distinguish among religions, even though we are fully aware that there are many major differences among them. Why have we done this? We draw a clear distinction between the specific beliefs associated with particular religions and the underlying psychological processes that lead to adherence to various religions. We totally accept that there are very large differences among the world's major religions in terms of specific beliefs. However, we argue that there are major commonalities among the world's major religions with respect to the psychological factors leading individuals to adhere to them.

ARE RELIGIOUS BELIEFS ASSOCIATED WITH PARANORMAL BELIEFS?

Our starting point in the search for important psychological differences between religious believers and non-believers is to consider whether they differ with respect to various paranormal beliefs. In view of the presence of this chapter in a book on parapsychology, you would probably guess (correctly!) that the two groups do differ in that believers are more likely than non-believers to have paranormal beliefs.

Bannerjee and Bloom found that individuals who believe in God are far more likely than those who don't believe in God to have a range of paranormal beliefs. The obvious follow-up question is to ask why this is the case. Bannerjee and Bloom came up with the interesting hypothesis that individuals who have strong religious and paranormal beliefs may have an exaggerated tendency to perceive the world as being governed by an underlying sense of purpose.

Bannerjee and Bloom tested their hypothesis by asking people to imagine themselves experiencing various important life events. Here is an example:

> Imagine that you are planning on travelling across the country for a very important business meeting. On the morning of your trip,

you accidentally sleep through your alarm clock and miss your flight. Later that day, you learn that the plane you were scheduled to be on crashed just after take-off with no survivors.

For each hypothetical life event, people were asked to indicate the extent to which they believed fate was responsible for causing it. The key findings were that those with religious beliefs and those with paranormal beliefs were much more likely than those without such beliefs to attribute what happened to fate or an underlying sense of purpose.

You may be wondering whether it really makes sense to categorise everyone as a religious believer or non-believer. There are many parts of the world (such as the West Coast of the United States and Canada) where there are literally millions of individuals who regard themselves as being "spiritual but not religious". For example, a recent newspaper poll found that 27% of Canadians who regarded themselves as atheists or agnostics nevertheless claimed to be "spiritual".

When those who are spiritual but not religious were compared against religious believers and non-believers, their tendency to hold paranormal beliefs was somewhat greater than that of religious believers and much stronger than non-believers. They also scored higher than the other two groups on most supernatural beliefs and experiences. Speculatively, an important reason why many individuals prefer to be spiritual without religion rather than simply being religious is that religion is somewhat constraining in terms of expectations as to what individuals can and should believe. In other words, being spiritual but not religious may appeal to those who pride themselves on being "free spirits" (no pun intended!).

We have established that religious believers (as well as individuals who are spiritual but not religious) are far more likely than religious non-believers to hold various paranormal beliefs. What we need to do next is to try to understand why that is the case. At a very general level, the association between religious and paranormal beliefs can be explained in a positive or a negative way. According to a positive interpretation, those with religious and paranormal beliefs are open-minded individuals whose minds are not constrained by rationality and who emphasise the importance of emotional experience. This interpretation is consistent with the often-expressed notion that religious belief is a matter of faith and emotion rather than cold-blooded logic.

According to a negative interpretation, individuals who are naïve and/or gullible are more likely than other people to hold religious and paranormal beliefs. As we will see shortly, the actual reasons are more complex than implied by either of these interpretations. Before we focus on such issues, we will briefly consider some of the reasons motivating religious belief.

RELIGIOUS MOTIVATION

It is commonly believed that religion thrives among people who are living in very deprived and difficult circumstances. This notion was perhaps expressed most vividly by the American military chaplain William Cummings. He proclaimed, "There are no atheists in foxholes" (a foxhole is a hole in the ground providing extremely limited protection from enemy gunfire). As scientists, we are vividly aware that many common beliefs turn out to be entirely wrong when subjected to experimental test. For example, there was a time when nearly everyone believed that the earth was flat and that the sun revolves around the earth. Accordingly, it is worth spending a little time considering the evidence to see whether it is really true that deprivation fosters religious belief.

It turns out that the expectation that religious believers are much more numerous in poor than in wealthy countries is convincingly supported by the evidence. Barber and his colleagues carried out a study of over one hundred countries. They discovered that religious views were especially strong in relatively poor countries where income inequality was the greatest. The American psychologist Ed Diener obtained similar findings. He also shed light on why this is the case. In poor countries, possessing strong religious beliefs was associated with enhanced subjective well-being, and this association was influenced by factors such as social support, purpose or meaning in life, and feeling respected.

In wealthy countries, in contrast, possessing religious beliefs had a rather modest beneficial effect on subjective well-being. Why was that the case? According to Ed Diener, the main reason is that even most non-religious individuals in such countries generally have fairly high levels of social support and respect as well as subjective well-being.

We can pursue some of the ideas discussed above by focusing on the effects of loneliness on religious beliefs. John Cacioppo investigated this issue, having started with the uncontroversial assumption that loneliness motivated individuals to create social connections. Individuals who were chronically lonely (or who had been induced to feel lonely) had stronger religious beliefs than those who were not lonely. They were also more likely to attribute human-like attributes (e.g. considerate; thoughtful; sympathetic) to pets.

MODES OF THINKING

Psychologists have discovered that relatively intelligent individuals often (but by no means always) engage in more analytic or reflective thinking than other individuals. Are there any reasons why we might expect religious believers to differ from non-believers with respect to intelligence and analytic thinking? Since the evidence strongly suggests that religious belief stems from faith rather than lengthy analytic thinking, we might speculatively (and controversially!) predict that religious believers would be somewhat less intelligent than non-believers and to use analytic thinking less often than non-believers. Dozens of studies have focused on the relationship between religious belief and intelligence. The findings are somewhat variable. However, on average, there is a modest tendency for non-believers to be more intelligent than religious believers.

The association between religious belief and measures of analytic thinking was recently assessed across a total sample of over 15,000 individuals. The researchers discovered that there is fairly modest negative relationship between religious belief and analytic thinking ability. Among non-believers, atheists on average exhibited more analytic thinking ability than agnostics.

In view of the links we have discussed between religious and paranormal beliefs, we might expect that individuals who have strong paranormal beliefs should on average have less analytic thinking ability than those with weak or no paranormal beliefs. That is, indeed, the case. By the way, good analytic thinking ability provides a good defence against bullshit. Researchers developed a Bullshit Receptivity scale that included statements such as the following: (1) "Consciousness is the growth of coherence, and of us"; (2) "We are in the midst of a self-aware blossoming of being that will align us with the nexus itself"; and (3) "Wholeness quiets infinite phenomena". Those with high analytic thinking ability were more likely than other people to realise the meaninglessness of these and other similar statements.

We have seen that religious believers on average have slightly lower analytic thinking ability and intelligence than non-believers. How should we interpret these findings? One possibility is simply that religious believers are (as suggested earlier) more naïve and gullible than non-believers. However, as we will see shortly, that is by no means the entire story. We also need to focus on non-believers so that we can identify some of the reasons why they are resistant to religious doctrine and faith.

PERCEIVED CONTROL

Most human beings are highly motivated to perceive the world as orderly even when that is not objectively the case. Indeed, the motivation to believe in a non-random (and just) world is so strong that Melvin Lerner called it our "fundamental delusion". Why are we susceptible to this delusion? Perhaps the most important reason is that a lack of perceived control is a major determinant of anxiety.

In a classic study, David Barlow and his colleagues exposed panic disorder patients to carbon dioxide in air. Some of these patients were given potential control over the concentration of carbon dioxide, whereas others had no control. Even though none of the patients with potential control exerted it, they had lower levels of self-reported anxiety and fewer symptoms than those without control. The most striking finding was that patients with perceived control were far less likely than those without perceived control to experience a panic attack (20% vs. 80%, respectively). Thus, perceived control (even when this control if not used) can produce substantial reductions in anxiety.

Kay et al. proposed an interesting theoretical approach to understanding religious and paranormal beliefs. The essence of their approach (entirely consistent with what has been said so far) was expressed as follows by Kay et al.: "To insulate themselves from the disabling anxiety that perceptions of randomness incite, individuals psychologically imbue their social, physical, and metaphysical environments with order and structure". It follows from this approach that individuals lacking perceived control over their lives may develop religious beliefs because such beliefs provide them with compensatory control.

We can develop the line of argument above. There are two main ways individuals can use compensatory control to reduce the anxiety that is associated with a random world. First, those individuals with the necessary resources or motivation (e.g. high intelligence; strong social connections) focus on *internal* personal control. Second, those individuals lacking such resources focus on *external* sources of control – believing in the existence of a controlling God convinces them the world is not random or chaotic.

Suppose we consider individuals exposed to a natural disaster such as the major earthquake close to Christchurch, New Zealand at 12:51 on 22 February 2011. This earthquake led to the deaths of 185 people and left several thousand people seriously injured. We would obviously expect that this disaster would have led to a loss of perceived control by those in the vicinity. As predicted by Kay et al.'s theoretical approach, those directly affected showed a significant increase in religious commitment.

Some of the ideas we have been discussing can help to shed light on the views of approximately 50% of Americans concerning the origins of human life and the universe. These Americans prefer an explanation in terms of intelligent design (i.e. everything was created and designed by an intelligent entity) rather than Darwin's theory of evolution. In some ways it seems hard to explain this preference, given that there is no empirical support for intelligent design, whereas there is possibly more support for Darwin's theory than any other scientific theory. Ironically, there is much evidence that the design of humans is less than intelligent in various ways. For example, we are much more prone to colds than most other mammalian species, because we need a very varied diet to provide us with the vitamins we need. Also, our knees are prone to problems because they are not well suited to walking and running on two legs.

Part of the reason why tens of millions of Americans reject Darwin's theory of evolution is because it apparently emphasises a fairly random process that is strongly influenced by unpredictable environmental changes (e.g. large meteors hitting the Earth's surface). Note, however, that Darwin's views on the evolutionary process imply less randomness than is often assumed. Mutations may occur in a random fashion. However, what determines whether any given mutation becomes established in subsequent generations is whether it facilitates survival and reproduction – this is not a random process at all.

In contrast to Darwin's apparent emphasis on randomness, the notion of intelligent design postulates a controlling designer. As a consequence, individuals' perceived control is greater with this latter explanation. It follows that individuals whose level of perceived control was experimentally reduced would be less enthusiastic about Darwin's theory than those with high levels of perceived control. That is precisely what has been found.

We could test ideas about the importance of perceived control more thoroughly if we could find a version of Darwin's theory of evolution that differs from it in claiming that the entire process of evolution has been somewhat orderly and predictable rather than random. Conveniently, Professor Simon Conway Morris, a palaeontologist at Cambridge University, has proposed just such a theory. In essence, he argues the notion of convergence – evolutionary processes can arrive at the same biological solution even though the starting positions were very different. Strikingly, close study of the fossil records indicates that birds have evolved at least twice and possibly three or four times!

What would we expect to find if individuals whose level of perceived control was experimentally reduced chose between Conway Morris' version of evolution and the Darwinian original? The most plausible prediction is that they would prefer Conway Morris' version and would do so to a greater extent than individuals whose level of perceived control had not been reduced. That is precisely what was found to be the case. The take-home message is that individuals lacking perceived control are motivated to regard the world as orderly and non-random, and this goal can be achieved by religious or non-religious means.

We have seen that deficient perceived control often increases the tendency to espouse religious beliefs. Researchers have also explored the role of perceived control in irrational beliefs such as precognition (the ability to predict the future) and obtained rather similar findings. Approximately 25% of Americans believe in precognition, agreeing with absurd statements such as, "Astrology is a way to accurately predict the future". Greenaway and her colleagues carried out several studies of perceived control and belief in precognition. In one study, individuals' perceived control was manipulated by instructing them to recall and then write about a time when they felt in control or had no control. The key finding was that perceived loss of control enhanced precognition beliefs. In another study, Greenaway manipulated beliefs in precognition. Those individuals whose belief in precognition had been increased by reading a text indicating that precognition exists reported higher perceived control. In a third study, Greenaway and her colleagues obtained evidence that, when individuals lacked control, believing in precognition assisted them to regain a sense of control.

MENTALISING AND RELIGIOUS BELIEFS

One of the most important differences between humans and the members of most (or possibly all) other species is that we often engage in what is often known as mentalising. Mentalising is basically the ability to infer (and also to think about) the mental states of individuals other than ourselves. What is the relevance of this to religious beliefs? An intriguing possibility is that religious believers use mentalising to think about (and to interact with) God.

One approach we can take to test the ideas presented in the previous paragraph is by using a magnetic resonance imaging (MRI) scanner to assess patterns of brain activity in various situations. Our starting point is the finding that mentalising in everyday life is associated with activation in three main brain areas: anterior medial prefrontal cortex, temporo-polar region, and temporo-parietal junction. Intriguingly, these same three brain areas were found to be strongly activated when religious individuals conversed with a personal God. This suggests that praying to God involves very similar processes to those involved in interpersonal interaction. In another study, these three brain areas were also activated when religious believers thought about God's mental states (especially anger).

There is another way we could test the notion that mentalising plays a key role in religious beliefs, namely, by predicting that individuals lacking mentalising ability would be unable to conceptualise supernatural agencies such as God. Individuals with autistic spectrum disorder have very poor mentalising ability and so find it very hard to understand the thoughts and intentions of others. More generally, this condition is associated with great problems in communicating and interacting with others.

From what has been said so far, we would expect relatively few individuals with autistic spectrum disorder to believe in God. The evidence mostly supports that expectation. For example, it was found in a relatively recent American study that autistic adolescents in Florida were only 11% as likely as adolescent controls to claim strong beliefs in God. It also emerged in this study that the single most important reason why the great majority of adolescents did not believe in God was because they lacked mentalising ability.

The assumption that mentalising plays an important role in believers' interactions with God allows us to make various additional predictions. For example, it has been found repeatedly that most of us are more likely to engage in prosocial behaviour (e.g. helping, cooperating; sharing; comforting) when we think other people are monitoring or observing our behaviour. We might expect to obtain similar findings when individuals possessing religious beliefs are primed with thoughts of God and religion. As predicted, such priming caused religious believers to show greater honesty, generosity, and fairness.

Presumably mentalising about God increases prosocial behaviour because religious believers think their behaviour is being monitored. This suggests the intriguing possibility that we could enhance prosocial behaviour by persuading individuals to engage in mentalising about some other supernatural agent. Indeed, one study has shown that when people heard about the ghost of a deceased graduate student, this was sufficient to make them less likely to cheat!

We can think of the effect on religious believers of thinking about God as being similar to being observed by a "camera in the sky". How can we test that idea? Much research has shown that individuals with a video camera pointing at them experience increased public self-awareness (i.e. they focus their attention on themselves). Interestingly, thinking about God has been found to increase the public self-awareness of Christians with strong religious beliefs to the same extent as thinking about being judged by other people.

BEYOND MENTALISING

We have seen that we can obtain partial understanding of why some individuals have religious beliefs whereas others do not by focusing on individual differences in mentalising ability. However, that is clearly only part of what is involved. There are approximately half a billion atheists worldwide, and only a very small fraction of them have serious problems with their mentalising ability. This means that the ability to mentalise may be necessary for someone to have religious beliefs but it is obviously not sufficient.

What factors other than mentalising ability do we need to consider to account for religious beliefs? An interesting starting point is to assume that religious beliefs do not depend on or involve cognitive processes that are unique or specific to religion but rather that these cognitive processes are commonly used in everyday life.

Numerous suggestions have been put forward as to the nature of the cognitive processes leading to religious beliefs. Here we will discuss two of the most important of such factors. First, there is mind–body dualism, which is the notion that minds can operate separately or independently of physical bodies. Second, there are teleological beliefs, which is the notion that animals, natural objects, and artefacts exist for a purpose. Canadian–American psychologist Paul Bloom has suggested that religion is a by-product of these beliefs. It is certainly true (as Jean Piaget and other developmental psychologists discovered a long time ago) that young children are virtually all dualists and teleologists. Children are very prone to teleological beliefs, believing that numerous animals, artefacts, and natural objects exist for a given purpose. For example, many children believe rocks are pointy so that animals will not sit on them.

There are various reasons why mind–body dualism and teleological beliefs might be associated with religious beliefs. Mind–body dualism can easily lead to a belief in disembodied intentional agents such as God or spirits. Teleological beliefs are consistent with the notion that the universe and all the creatures within it have been created by a God through purposeful design.

It has been discovered that a belief in mind–body dualism is a strong predictor of religious beliefs. Teleological beliefs are also associated with religious beliefs but to a lesser extent. Of relevance, individuals who have religious beliefs were more likely than non-believers to explain events in their own lives in teleological terms.

So far, we have assumed implicitly that there are no real links between mentalising ability, on the one hand, and mind–body dualism and teleological beliefs, on the other hand. There is recent intriguing evidence that that assumption is false and that mind–body dualism and teleological beliefs depend on mentalising ability. For example, researchers in one study asked religious believers, atheists, and individuals with Asperger's syndrome (a form of high-functioning autism characterised by mentalising deficits) to discuss the significance of two significant life events they had experienced. The key finding was that those with Asperger's syndrome provided fewer teleological explanations of these life events than either the religious believers or the atheists.

Additional insights into mind–body dualism and teleological beliefs can be obtained by considering these beliefs in the context of recent theories of thinking and reasoning within cognitive psychology. Remember that we earlier discussed evidence showing that religious believers are less likely than non-believers to engage in analytic or deliberate thinking. In recent years, it has become increasingly popular for cognitive psychologists to propose theories assuming that there is a crucially important distinction between such slow, deliberate, analytic processes and rapid, 'automatic', intuitive processes. The best-known advocate of the dual-process approach is Danny Kahneman, who won the Nobel Prize for Economics in 2002. In his 2011 book, *Thinking, Fast and Slow*, he provided a popular account of this theoretical approach.

Are beliefs in mind–body dualism and teleological beliefs associated more with rapid intuitive processes or with slow analytic processes? As we have seen, these beliefs are very strong in young children. These beliefs also represent incorrect ways of thinking. These two facts together suggest the hypothesis that they are both associated with rapid intuitive processes. Two predictions follow from this hypothesis:

1 Individuals should be more prone to such beliefs when their available cognitive resources are reduced experimentally.
2 The strength of such beliefs should be reduced when individuals are persuaded to make increased use of analytic processes. As a rider to this prediction, note that earlier we discussed evidence suggesting that holding religious beliefs tends to be associated with relatively little use of analytic processes. This suggests the intriguing prediction that religious beliefs might also be reduced if people engaged more in analytic processes.

Let's start with the first prediction. In one study, university students decided whether various statements were correct. Of most immediate relevance here were sentences including unwarranted teleological explanations (e.g. "The sun radiates heat because warmth nurtures life"; "Eyelashes developed so that people can wear mascara"). When the students were required to respond rapidly (and so had reduced ability to use analytic processes), they incorrectly accepted significantly more unwarranted teleological explanations than when they had more time available.

Suppose we studied the tendency of professional physicists to endorse false teleological beliefs of natural phenomena (e.g. "Lamps shine brightly so they can produce light"). We would expect that they would very rarely subscribe to such false beliefs in their area of expertise, even when their ability to use analytic processing was severely reduced by the requirement to respond rapidly. In fact, however, professional physicists had a 15% endorsement rate for false teleological beliefs when they had ample time to respond and this almost doubled to 29% when they had to respond rapidly.

It is now time to turn to the second prediction mentioned earlier. Support for this prediction was reported by Gervais and Norenzayan in a study in which they made use of various manipulations to enhance analytic processing. They found that these manipulations temporarily decreased religious beliefs, suggesting such beliefs are anchored in intuitive processes. Of course, numerous other factors (e.g. the cultural context) also influence the presence or absence of religious beliefs.

So far, we have discussed intuitive and analytic processes as if they were totally independent. In fact, that is often not the case. Instead, analytic processes often monitor the responses produced by intuitive processing and sometimes inhibit them. There is some evidence that such inhibitory processes are stronger in religious non-believers than in believers. This may help to explain why non-believers are relatively unaffected by beliefs (e.g. teleological beliefs; mind–body dualism beliefs) produced by intuitive processes.

HOW CAN WE DESCRIBE GOD?

It is true of most religious believers that they have a conceptualisation of the God or gods in whom they believe. How can we explain their conceptualisations? The ancient Greek philosopher, theologian, and poet Xenophanes of Colophon claimed these conceptualisations are strongly influenced by the ways we conceptualise human beings. Here is the essence of his approach:

> But mortals suppose that gods are born,
> wear their own clothes and have a voice and body . . .
> Ethiopians say that their gods are snub-nosed and black;
> Thracians that theirs are blue-eyed and red-haired . . .
> But if horses or oxen or lions had hands
> or could draw with their hands and accomplish such works as men,
> horses would draw the figures of the gods as similar to horses, and the oxen
> as similar to oxen, and they would make the bodies
> of the sort which each of them had.

The essence of Xenophanes' viewpoint is simple: basically, religious believers create God in their own image. This is, of course, the opposite direction of causality to that stated in Genesis: "God created man in His own image". Approximately two thousand years after Xenophanes, the French philosopher Voltaire provided a very famous quotation supporting his view: "If God created us in His own image, we have more than reciprocated".

Barrett and Keil tested the Xenophanes–Voltaire viewpoint. Religious students read a story in which God was NOT described in human-like terms. After that, they reconstructed the story. The key finding was that the reconstructed story differed from the original version in that God had human-like limitations absent from the original. For example, some students misremembered the story as stating that God needed perceptual information to know about events or that he could perform only one action at a time.

We can extend the notion that religious believers' conceptualisations of God are strongly influenced by human characteristics to explain their views concerning God's beliefs. Our starting point here is that, for most of us, our beliefs concerning another person's beliefs are influenced by egocentric processes. What that means is that we tend to assume that other people's beliefs are more similar to our own than is actually the case.

Epley et al. carried out a series of experiments to test whether religious believers' reasoning about God's beliefs also exhibited egocentricity. In one experiment, they obtained evidence that religious believers show a greater egocentric bias with respect to their assessment of God's beliefs than those of another person. More specifically, brain areas associated with thinking about oneself and one's own views were more activated when religious believers focused on God's beliefs than when they focused on another person's beliefs.

Epley et al. went on to obtain even stronger evidence that religious believers are especially likely to use their own beliefs when reasoning about God's beliefs compared to reasoning about other people's beliefs. What they did was manipulate religious believers' own beliefs on various political and moral issues such as abortion, same-sex marriage, and affirmative action to enhance the prospects of minority groups. These manipulations were successful and subsequently changed religious believers' estimates of God's beliefs more than it changed their estimates of other people's beliefs. This finding can be explained on the basis that religious believers typically have more direct evidence concerning the actual beliefs of other people than those of God.

What can we conclude? It is very often argued that God provides religious believers with a vital moral compass to guide them. Epley et al.'s findings suggest that, "unlike an actual compass, inferences about God's beliefs may instead move people further in whatever direction they are already facing". In other words, Voltaire was right!

PUTTING IT ALL TOGETHER

At a very general level, research on the psychology of religion has largely confirmed (and in many cases extended) the views on religion held by millions of those unfamiliar with the scientific evidence. For example, the research evidence is consistent with the common assumptions that an overwhelming majority of human beings have strong desires to be socially connected with other people, to love and to be loved, to discover that the world is an orderly and non-random place, and to perceive that they can control their environment. These are all basic motives. Individuals whose lives fail to satisfy one or more of these basic motives are more receptive than others to religion. The key reason is that religion potentially satisfies all these motives, and by so doing serves to provide religious individuals with a sense of purpose and meaning in life.

What is original and distinctive about the contribution that psychological research has made to our understanding of the reasons for religious belief? First, we have seen that the cognitive, social, and other processes associated with religious beliefs resemble those involved in other kinds of beliefs, including paranormal beliefs. Second, many (or most) of the processes associated with religious (and paranormal) beliefs are essentially by-products of processes that occur in everyday life.

Let us pursue the second point above. It is often assumed metaphorically that religious believers have "conversations" with God. However, the psychological research extends this notion considerably. Psychologists have found that the processes involved when believers pray and converse with God are remarkably similar to those involved when they have conversations with friends. In both cases, there is a systematic attempt to understand what the other person (or God) is thinking and feeling. People's behaviour when they believe themselves to be observed by God is also remarkably similar to their behaviour when they are observed by other people. Finally, the notion that religious believers have created God in their own image seems to be much closer to the truth than is generally realised.

In our everyday lives, we attach considerable importance to perceived control. When we actually lack control, we can sometimes nevertheless have perceived control by using rapid, intuitive processes (e.g. teleological beliefs; mind–body dualism beliefs) and avoiding slow, analytic processes. Similar processes involving belief in an all-seeing and all-knowing God provide religious believers with perceived control in their lives.

In sum, we have hopefully shed some light on some of the main social, emotional, and cognitive processes associated with religious belief. We leave deeper philosophical and moral issues relating to religion to those wiser than we are!

7

EXPLAINING PARANORMAL BELIEFS

David Groome, Michael Eysenck, and Robin Law

EVIDENCE FOR PARANORMAL EVENTS

If you have read the preceding chapters of this book, you will almost certainly have noticed that we were unable to find any convincing scientific evidence to confirm the occurrence of any of the widely reported paranormal phenomena that we have reviewed here. There have been many studies claiming to demonstrate the occurrence of paranormal phenomena, but none of them have really stood up to scientific investigation. In every case, the findings can be explained by poor experimental procedures, selective publication, or even downright cheating.

So, it seems that astrologers are unable to tell us anything useful about people from their birth dates, nor can they predict future events. Extra-sensory perception does not seem to work when tested under controlled scientific conditions. Mediums who claim to be able to communicate with the spirits of dead people cannot demonstrate this ability in front of scientists. And there is no convincing evidence to support any of the claims made by the alleged victims of alien abduction.

The lack of evidence for the occurrence of these paranormal phenomena may seem a little disappointing, but it does raise a very interesting question: why do so many people believe in the paranormal despite the lack of any supporting evidence? In fact, we can learn a great deal about the workings of the human mind by examining the reasons why so many people hold beliefs which are entirely unsupported by any kind of evidence. We will now discuss some of the possible explanations for these irrational beliefs, and what we can learn from them about the way peoples' minds work.

CHANCE, COINCIDENCE, AND PROBABILITY JUDGEMENTS

Strange and unexpected events and coincidences happen from time to time, and when they do it is a matter of personal judgement whether we attribute them to chance or to some other factor, such as paranormal influences. For example, you may find yourself thinking about a particular friend, only to have that same friend phone you shortly afterwards. Does this seem to you like a clear case of ESP, or was it just a coincidence? Or perhaps you read your horoscope in the newspaper one morning, and you find that it seems to fit quite well with the way your day actually turns out. Does this prove that the astrologer can accurately predict events, or do you dismiss it as simply a lucky guess? Suppose you met someone at a party who turned out to have the same birthday as you – would you consider that this went beyond coincidence and must be somehow fated or brought about by paranormal forces?

When a person experiences something mysterious, as in the above examples, they can either conclude that it must be the result of some paranormal influence or they can dismiss it as mere chance. Essentially, this involves making a judgement of probability. The person may decide that the probability of the event occurring by chance was sufficiently high as to require no further explanation, or that the event was so improbable that it could only be explained by paranormal forces of some kind. It has been found that people vary quite considerably in their ability to assess the probability of a particular event. There are some people who would dismiss all three of the examples above as mere chance or coincidence, whereas others would regard the same occurrences as going beyond any possible coincidence and thus requiring a paranormal explanation.

A study carried out by Susan Blackmore and Tom Troscianko in 1985 found that people who believe in paranormal phenomena tend to be less accurate in making probability judgements than non-believers. In particular, the believers were found to be more likely to underestimate the probability of an event occurring by chance. This could help to explain why they are more likely to assume that their experiences have a paranormal explanation, since they are more likely to regard an unusual event as being so improbable as to be beyond coincidence.

Blackmore and Troscianko presented their participants with a number of scenarios involving a coincidence or an unusual experience, and they were required to estimate the probability of this event occurring by chance. For example, one of their questions involved guessing the probability of meeting someone with the same birthday in a room full of people, as in the example mentioned earlier in this section. In fact, you would need only 23 people in the room to have a 50/50 chance of two of them sharing a birthday. Most people in the study tended to underestimate the chance of a shared birthday in such a group, but those who were paranormal believers thought that the chances were far lower, in fact almost zero. The believers were found to be bad at estimating probabilities in a number of different tasks, and in all cases their errors involved underestimating the likelihood of a particular occurrence. The people in the believers' group were therefore more likely to regard a fairly likely event as being highly improbable and thus beyond chance or coincidence. This could explain why paranormal believers often assume that paranormal forces are at work even when they are not.

One further mechanism that may make it more likely that a person will hang on to a paranormal belief even in the face of contradictory evidence is what psychologists call "confirmation bias". This term refers to a well-established finding that people attend to incoming information in a selective manner, and in particular they interpret such input on the basis of pre-existing beliefs. So, if you believe in astrology, then you will notice when the astrologer's column in your newspaper makes a correct prediction, but you won't pay as much attention to the predictions they get wrong. The result of such a confirmation bias is that people tend to stick rigidly to their beliefs and blindly ignore anything that might contradict them.

FALSE MEMORIES, SUGGESTIBILITY, AND FANTASY

In 2006, Krissy Wilson and Chris French carried out an experiment which showed that believers in the paranormal were more likely than non-believers to hold false memories (i.e. memories for experiences which seem real but which did not actually happen to them). For example, they asked their participants to recall whether they had watched TV footage of a number of news events, but they included one event (a nightclub bombing in Bali) for which no TV footage actually existed. Those who described seeing such news events on TV were therefore mistaken, and false memories of this kind occurred mainly among the paranormal believers.

There is also evidence that believers in the paranormal tend to be more vulnerable to suggestion than non-believers, as mentioned earlier in this book. For example, in 2003 Richard Wiseman and his colleagues arranged a fake séance during which they suggested to their participants that a table was rising into the air, though in reality it did not actually move. Some of their participants agreed that the table had moved, but others did not. It was found that those participants who were believers in the paranormal were more likely to report that the table had moved. In a similar experiment carried out in 2014, Wilson and French found that paranormal believers were more likely to be convinced by a suggestion that a key was bending even though it was not. The believers found the suggestion especially convincing when other members of the audience claimed that they had seen the key bend, indicating that believers were also more vulnerable to social pressure.

People who believe in the paranormal have also been found to be more prone to indulging in fantasy than the average person. In one such study carried out by Harvey Irwin in 1990, participants were asked to try to recall childhood memories. He found that paranormal believers had more difficulty than others in distinguishing real from imagined events, and they would often report having actually experienced an event when in fact they had imagined it. Irwin also found that both fantasy proneness and paranormal beliefs tend to be more prevalent in individuals who have suffered physical abuse in childhood. He suggests that abused individuals might use fantasy as a psychological coping mechanism, to help them to escape from the horrors of their real lives. Fantasy might also help victims of abuse to regain a sense of control over their lives, and to counteract the sense of helplessness generated by physical abuse.

SEEING FACES IN THE CLOUDS

All of us occasionally see faces or other familiar shapes in the clouds, or in a wallpaper pattern or some other fairly random array. Finding shapes and images in random patterns is a common experience in humans, and it simply reflects the normal way in which our brains make sense of their visual input by searching for familiar shapes and things they have experienced before. However, it has been found that some people are particularly prone to seeing familiar shapes in a pattern of random dots or lines, and recent studies by Swiss psychologist Peter Brugger have shown that these people are also more likely to be believers in the paranormal.

Identifying shapes and patterns in our sensory input is crucial to our ability to make sense of the world. Frederick Bartlett, an important early psychologist, demonstrated back in 1932 that stored patterns and shapes in the brain (which he called "schemas") were used to analyse our perceptual input, as a fundamental part of the perceptual process. However, the brain would be unable to process an unlimited number of meaningful patterns and images impinging on it at a given moment, so there are probably neural mechanisms at work which inhibit some of the weaker patterns. Brugger suggests that some people have weaker inhibition of schemas than others, so they will be more likely to find patterns and shapes in their perceptual input even for very weak schemas. Such individuals will therefore be more prone to finding meaningful shapes and patterns in their surroundings, even when the input is basically a random array. If you believe that you have detected something familiar and meaningful in a random pattern, then you will probably seek an explanation, and this could make a paranormal interpretation of events seem more likely. So, a group of distant street lamps could be mistakenly perceived as a flying saucer, and the rustling of leaves might sound like a spoken message from the gods or spirits of the departed. This view is largely speculative, but it is consistent with the finding that schizophrenics (who tend to experience delusions and hallucinations) are more likely to believe in the paranormal than the average person.

INTUITIVE AND ANALYTIC THINKING

From the evidence discussed above, it would appear that some people may be more prone to belief in the paranormal because of the way they interpret the perceptual input they receive from the outside world. Recent research has suggested that some individuals may be more prone to paranormal belief because they employ an "intuitive" rather than an "analytic" thinking style.

The distinction between these two types of thinking was first highlighted by Nobel prize-winner Daniel Kahneman in his 2011 book *Thinking, Fast and Slow*. He described intuitive thinking as involving an instinctive "gut reaction" to the input, relying on unconscious thought processes. In contrast, analytic thinking requires conscious thought, and it involves a more complex assessment of events. Analytical thinking is a slower process than intuition and requires more effort, but it is usually found to be less prone to error and a better way of forming logical conclusions.

In practice, most people employ both types of thinking when faced with a problem, and our immediate reaction is likely to be an intuitive one. However, some individuals tend to proceed from this to an analytical thought process, which allows us to reflect upon, and possibly dismiss, our earlier intuitions. However, there are other people who tend to rely more on their initial intuitive response, with little or no effort to carry out analytic thought. There is good evidence to show that people differ in the extent to which they rely on intuitive or analytical thought, and these differences have been shown to predict a wide range of beliefs and behavioural outcomes. Gordon Pennycook reported in 2011 that those who tend to adopt an analytic style of thinking are less likely to believe in the paranormal. So, the extent to which we are willing and able to engage in analytic thought may help to explain why some people are prone to belief in the paranormal and others are not. A lack of analytical thinking may reduce a person's ability to critically examine the evidence for paranormal phenomena.

THE BENEFITS OF BELIEVING

It seems likely that people who hold on to paranormal beliefs, despite the lack of any supporting evidence, might derive some benefit from holding those beliefs. Perhaps a belief in the paranormal makes people feel that they have more understanding and more control over the events of their lives. For example, if you believe in astrology, then you may think that you can predict future events and use this foreknowledge to make important decisions. You might also believe that astrology can provide you with insights into the personality and behaviour of others, which would give you an advantage in dealing with people, and it might also give you a sense of superiority over other people. If you believe that a medium can help you to communicate with the spirit of a deceased friend or relative, then you may find this comforting, almost as if you have not really lost them. Religious beliefs also offer comfort and reassurance, in a fairly similar way. Most religions teach that there is a benign God looking after us, and that after you die you will continue to dwell happily in the afterlife. For some people, a belief in the paranormal may offer an alternative to religious beliefs, as religious and paranormal beliefs do seem to offer similar benefits of comfort and reassurance.

SOME FINAL CONCLUSIONS

In summary, it has been found that believers in the paranormal are more prone to probability misjudgements, fantasising, false beliefs, finding familiar shapes in random arrays, and relying on intuitive rather than analytic thinking styles. A person who processes their perceptual input in these ways would be more likely to mistakenly attribute paranormal causes to experiences which actually have a normal explanation. These findings would therefore seem to offer a plausible explanation for the fact that some people believe in paranormal phenomena. However, while believers in the paranormal are more likely to make errors and misjudgements about their experiences, this does not necessarily mean that they are in some way inadequate or flawed individuals. Although they may make some mistakes as a result of their beliefs, they may benefit from the reassurance gained from perceiving life as being more predictable, and an increased sense of control over events. Perhaps we can regard them as people who see the world in a slightly different way to the average person. Great artists, writers, and musicians have been doing this since the beginning of time. But as scientists, we have to conclude that, so far, we have seen no convincing evidence for the occurrence of any paranormal phenomena. However, being scientists means that we will keep looking.